Praise for *Leadership Sh!t show*

Having just completed the journey through the book, I must express my deepest gratitude for the profound insights and inspiration it has bestowed upon me. Elena's words have illuminated a path of leadership that transcends time, offering invaluable guidance for the generations yet to come.

Reflecting on my own journey, I can't help but feel a twinge of regret that such wisdom wasn't accessible to me earlier in my career. Once the book is released, I will be among the first to purchase copies, ensuring that our company's future leaders and managers have access to its transformative message.

My wife and I have been blessed with incredibly supportive grandparents and parents, whose unwavering love and encouragement shaped who we are today. Elena's words have underscored the importance of fostering such an environment for our own children, and I am immensely proud of the values and work ethic they embody.

This book is a must-read for all those, regardless of background, who wish to transition to a leadership role in whatever activity they wish to pursue.

PATRICK PEARL, M.Eng, B.Eng(hons), FIEAust, SMIEEE, CPEng, NER, IntPE(Aus), RPEQ

In *Leadership Sh!t Show*, Elena Gosse presents a masterclass in leadership that is both inspiring and transformative. Elena, a mesmerising force and an inspiration to all who know her, has long been a trusted friend and colleague, guiding countless individuals and fellow spiritual warriors on their paths to success. As a leading Australian manufacturing CEO and a beacon of resilience, her insights in this book offer invaluable lessons for anyone seeking to elevate their leadership skills. I wholeheartedly encourage readers to dive into this remarkable work and learn from Elena's unparalleled experience and wisdom.

LISA LOCKLAND-BELL, Founder, Chief Executive Officer, Principal Vocal Coach, Performance Studios Australia

In *Leadership Sh!t Show*, Elena takes us on an extraordinary journey through the highs and lows of leadership. This book is a candid and inspiring exploration of what it means to lead in the face of adversity, culture shock and personal challenges.

From the very first chapter, where Elena recounts the tumultuous experience of divorce in Russia and subsequent move to Australia, the narrative is infused with humour, wisdom and unwavering resilience. Elena doesn't shy away from the messy reality of leadership and life. Instead, she embraces it, showing that real growth often comes from our most difficult experiences.

Elena's story of breaking through cultural and gender stereotypes in the swimming pool industry is particularly poignant and will resonate with a lot of readers. It serves as a powerful reminder that true leadership is about asserting one's identity and capabilities, even in the face of systemic biases and personal setbacks. Elena offers her insights into the importance of self-care and support systems in leadership. This is one of the many lessons I've learned from her and apply in my life today.

This book is rich with tools for self-reflection, goal setting, and adopting a growth mindset, making it a valuable resource for anyone looking to evolve as a leader. Leadership is not just about personal success; it's about the positive impact one can make on the broader community. The narrative's blend of humour and deep personal reflection makes the journey of leadership not only insightful but also deeply human and relatable.

EMMAGNESS RUZVIDZO, Award-winning brand strategist and personal branding coach Queensland's 40 Under 40

Elena's journey from adversity and challenge to success and recognition is truly inspirational. Having worked with Elena, this book authentically captures her integrity, drive, passion, and positive outlook on life. Each challenge she faces becomes a stepping stone to growth, reflecting her entrepreneurial spirit. This approach has earned her numerous accolades and deep respect within the business community. Elena is a genuine, heart-led leader who seeks to inspire, develop and uplift everyone around her, fostering a culture of engagement and growth.

ANTHONY THOMAS, FCPA

Leadership Sh!t Show by Elena Gosse is an insightful exploration of the tumultuous yet rewarding journey of leadership. Gosse's narrative intertwines personal growth with leadership, illustrating that true leadership is about authenticity and continuous self-improvement.

Overall, *Leadership Sh!t Show* is a candid, humorous and practical guide for anyone navigating the complex world of leadership, offering tools and insights to turn challenges into opportunities for growth.

JON LINDSAY, Chair, Vistage Australia

Where others failed, Elena Gosse succeeded. Where others gave up, she became more determined. Where others said no, she said, 'Absolutely yes!' It's impossible not to be carried along by her enthusiasm and determination, which comes in support of others, not at their expense. Elena's personal adversities have equipped her with the ability to reflect, transform and grow. In sharing her story, Elena distils the winning strategies that everyone can practise, no matter how strong the headwinds.

CHERYL GRAY, Chief Executive Officer, Women's Network Australia

One of the best books I have ever read! *Leadership Sh!t Show* tells the inspiring story of the incredible Elena Gosse. From humble beginnings in the Soviet Union to becoming one of the most awarded women in Australia, Elena has faced and overcome numerous adversities and challenges, shaping her into the remarkable woman she is today.

Her relentless determination and passion for helping others are just a few of her outstanding traits. This is a truly remarkable and unique story. If you are looking to be inspired by someone who has faced and conquered significant challenges, this book is for you!

JASON FONG, Director, Forbes Club at Forbes Australia

An extraordinary journey awaits within the pages of this book. Elena's captivating storytelling and profound insights make it a must-read for anyone seeking guidance, inspiration, and a good dose of laughter along the way. It has been an absolute honour to know Elena, and her book is a true reflection of her wisdom, heart-centred leadership, compassion and commitment to life-long learning. Through her words, Elena opens our minds to new perspectives, and challenges us to lead with empathy and belief in others. Each chapter is a testament to the power of resilience and the beauty of embracing life's twists and turns. Whether you're navigating personal growth, seeking solace in turbulent times, or simply looking for a refreshing perspective on leadership and life, this book offers invaluable support and encouragement.

BIRGIT SCHNELLE, Professional EOS Implementer® at EOS Worldwide

Elena Gosse is one of the most remarkable people I know. Her story is inspiring, uplifting and a great read! I can't wait to see the movie!

KENNETH BECK, Co-Founder & Chief Executive Officer, CEO Connection

LEADERSHIP
SH!T
SHOW

A VISIONARY LEADER'S PERSPECTIVE
ON THE CONTINUOUS
CYCLE OF LIFELONG GROWTH

BY ELENA GOSSE

GRAMMAR
FACTORY
— EST· 2013 —

Published by Grammar Factory Publishing, an imprint of MacMillan
Company Limited.

Grammar Factory Publishing
MacMillan Company Limited
25 Telegram Mews, 39th Floor, Suite 3906
Toronto, Ontario, Canada
M5V 3Z1

www.grammarfactory.com

Gosse, Elena
Leadership Sh!t Show: A Visionary Leader's Perspective on the
Continuous Cycle of Lifelong Growth / Elena Goose.

Paperback ISBN 978-1-998756-88-9
Hardcover ISBN 978-1-998756-90-2
eBook ISBN 978-1-998756-89-6

1. BUS071000 BUSINESS & ECONOMICS / Leadership. 2. BUS107000
BUSINESS & ECONOMICS / Personal Success 3. BUS046000
BUSINESS & ECONOMICS / Motivational.Production Credits

Production Credits
Cover design by Designerbility
Interior layout design by Setareh Ashrafologhalai
Book production and editorial services by Grammar Factory Publishing

Grammar Factory's Carbon Neutral Publishing Commitment
Grammar Factory Publishing is proud to be neutralizing the carbon
footprint of all printed copies of its authors' books printed by or
ordered directly through Grammar Factory or its affiliated companies
through the purchase of Gold Standard-Certified International Offsets.

Disclaimer
The material in this publication is of the nature of general comment
only and does not represent professional advice. It is not intended to
provide specific guidance for particular circumstances, and it should
not be relied on as the basis for any decision to take action or not take
action on any matter which it covers. Readers should obtain professional advice where appropriate, before making any such decision.
To the maximum extent permitted by law, the author and publisher
disclaim all responsibility and liability to any person, arising directly
or indirectly from any person taking or not taking action based on the
information in this publication..

For all the brave souls in leadership roles—
whether you're leading a company or your own life—
this one is for you. May your coffee be strong, your
meetings be short, and your sh!t shows be less frequent.

To those who see every leadership challenge as an
opportunity in disguise (a very, very good disguise)—here's
to finding the humour and growth in the journey.

For everyone who's ever thought, 'Is it just me, or is this a sh!t
show?'—you are not alone. Welcome to the club.

To those battling the sleepless nights, the endless
meetings, and the 'What now?' moments—you are the
true heroes of the chaos, and this book is for you.

And finally, to all who feel like they are swimming
upstream without a paddle—here's your floatie. Enjoy the
ride and know you have a trusted friend in these pages.

CONTENTS

FOREWORD

HEN I FIRST encountered Elena Gosse through my own work with Women's Legal Service Queensland, I was struck by the depth of her insights and the passion with which she approached community work. In a world filled with noise and distractions, Elena's voice rises above, clear and resonant, offering those who encounter her a pathway to understanding and enlightenment. As I continued to be exposed to Elena's work as the CEO and business owner of AIS Water, I was struck by her depth of character and her ability to lead large and diverse groups of people through difficult times, difficult subject matter, and groups of people who on the face of it appeared to have such different interests to her own.

I truly believe it is her tenacity to overcome adversity, her inability to simply walk with the herd, and her overwhelming ability to find the joy in everything around her which has led her to beat the odds not just because they told her she 'could not' or 'would not' but because no one was ever going to get in her way. And if they did, she was always going to find a way around them, because Elena lives her life with such authenticity that she creates and invests in the community around her—leading it to be a better place, perhaps by osmosis or perhaps because her positivity is infectious.

In this remarkable book, Elena invites us to explore the intricacies of her mind and the beauty of her perspective. Through her words, she weaves together a tapestry of wisdom, drawing from her rich experiences and profound reflections. Each page is an invitation to delve deeper into the complexities of life, to embrace its challenges with courage and grace, and to do it while navigating and avoiding burnout, something that plagues so many of us in a time where we are unable to switch off, required to be on and all while never admitting we are struggling.

Elena's reflections on leadership are profound and timely. In a world where effective leadership is often elusive, Elena offers a refreshing perspective that emphasises the importance of empathy, integrity and vision. Through her own experiences as a leader, she demonstrates the transformative power of compassionate leadership, showing us that true strength lies not in authority, but in service to others. Her insights remind us that leadership is not merely about wielding power or making decisions, but about inspiring and empowering those around us to reach their full potential. In a time marked by uncertainty and change, Elena's wisdom serves as a guiding beacon, reminding us of the crucial role that leadership plays in shaping the future of our communities and our world.

As I read Elena's book, I couldn't help but marvel at Elena's ability to capture the essence of human existence with such clarity and insight. Her words have a way of reaching into the depths of our souls, stirring emotions, and igniting a spark of introspection within us. But perhaps what truly sets Elena apart is her unwavering optimism and her belief in the power of the human spirit to overcome adversity. In a world that often feels divided and uncertain, Elena's message is one of hope and resilience, reminding us that even in our darkest moments, there is always light to guide us forward. She goes even further, giving her readers a step-by-step process to navigate the hard, insurmountable and plain difficult, providing insights on just how to rise from the ashes and keep soaring no matter where life takes us.

It is my sincere hope that readers will find inspiration and solace within these pages, just as I have.

DOMINIQUE LAMB, Queensland Small Business Commissioner

INTRODUCTION
WELCOME TO THE SH!T SHOW

A FEW YEARS AGO, an invitation to a leadership retreat on Necker Island with Sir Richard Branson set my world alight with excitement. I was so buoyed by the prospect that I couldn't contain my enthusiasm. 'I'm off to a leadership gathering,' I'd proclaim, 'ready to enhance my leadership skills!' I was all about 'leadership this, leadership that', until a curious interruption made me pause. 'Sorry, Elena, but what's this "leadersh!t" you keep mentioning?' It dawned on me then—my accent was betraying my intent! I thought I was saying 'leadership', but in my thick accent it sounded like 'leadersh!t'. Mortified yet amused, I sought the expertise of an opera singer friend who was also my vocal coach. She advised, 'Elena, just say it slowly: Lead-a-ship.' And then it clicked! Leaders do captain their ships, guiding their crew through a safe and rewarding journey, steering clear of icebergs. No one wants to become the captain of a Titanic.

But leadership isn't always smooth sailing. It's messy, challenging and yes, sometimes it feels like 'leadersh!t'. And that's exactly what I embraced. I decided to reclaim and reinvent the term. Because, let's face it, as leaders, we occasionally find ourselves in the thick of leadersh!t.

The Australian penchant for the word 'sh!t' in various contexts—from expressing almost anything from awe to frustration—resonated with me. It's versatile, expressive and undeniably human. And when it comes to leadership, being in the 'sh!t' isn't necessarily a bad place. It's where we're tested, where innovation and discovery thrive, and where we summon our inner strength for necessary changes.

This realisation led to an epiphany: becoming a successful leader often involves moving from leadersh!t to leading a shift before leading a ship. It's about embracing the mess, facing what's not working, and innovatively steering towards positive change. This shift is liberating, akin to shedding unnecessary weight, and essential for growth and learning.

Sharing this concept with friends, colleagues and even strangers, I was met with a unanimous response: 'You need to write a book about this.' The idea of penning a book was daunting; I was not an author. Yet, the encouragement planted a seed that eventually found the right moment to sprout.

So, without further ado, I'd like to say, 'Welcome to the Sh!t Show,' a term I use affectionately to describe the rollercoaster ride of leadership and life. This book isn't just a recount of my journey through family violence, a heart-wrenching divorce, and a bold leap into unfamiliar territory; it's a reflection on the resilience, humour and grit that transformed every hurdle I experienced into a stepping stone towards something greater.

In *Leadership Sh!t Show*, I'll take you beyond the facade of success to explore the often messy reality of leading and living with authenticity. Like you, I've navigated my fair share of leadership challenges—those moments when everything feels out of sync, like wearing the wrong shoes on the wrong feet. Here, success is not a static destination, but a dynamic, ever-evolving journey.

This book is more than a collection of stories. It's a guide through the trials and tribulations of leadership, a roadmap for making significant shifts, and a celebration of the moments when we truly take the helm of our lives. It's the journey of personal evolution I wish I had embarked on sooner, one that would have spared me countless tears and heartaches.

As your ally, this book will shed light on how to enhance relationships, foster authenticity, and see life's challenges as markers on the path to greater achievements. With each page, you'll gain insights to shift perspectives, gracefully handle life's curveballs and, most importantly, embrace your true self.

Be warned, though—this is no quick fix or trendy manual. If you're invested in maintaining appearances, the unvarnished truths within these pages might take you by surprise. But if you're holding this book, it's likely to be because you're ready to embark on a significant journey, and are resilient enough to face formidable challenges and emerge stronger on the other side. *Leadership Sh!t Show* explores introspection, growth and transformation, and offers tools to navigate your unique path to success and address the big questions that define your life.

So, congratulations on taking the first step towards change by embracing vulnerability and honesty. This is where you start to shift gears and reclaim control of your destiny. By facing your unresolved challenges head-on, you'll build confidence, courageously accept life's trials and transform them into triumphs.

Change is the only constant, and now it's time to set your course. I'm here to show you that with determination, the right mindset and unwavering persistence, anything is possible. I've weathered my sh!t show, and now I'm here to help you navigate yours. Let's embark on this journey together, turning our trials into a testament to the enduring power of growth and resilience.

My hope is to take you on a journey that not only unveils new perspectives, but also enriches your life, pushing you towards your full potential. True leadership is a continuous journey of learning. It's about embracing a mindset of perpetual improvement, and making that your second skin. Let's embark on this voyage together, navigate the tumultuous yet rewarding seas of leadership, and emerge as captains of our destiny.

CHAPTER I

MY SH!T SHOW— FROM RUSSIA FOR LOVE

TOOK MY FIRST breath in the heart of the Soviet Union during the tumultuous 1960s, when the country was still recovering from the Second World War and the Cold War cast a long shadow. The Soviet Union was a place where conformity was the anthem and individuality a foreign concept. As a spirited young girl with dreams bigger than the Red Square, I joined the Pioneer movement, an organisation for children operated by the communist party. Proudly wearing my red neckerchief, I marched through my childhood and adolescence under a red flag, drumming and blowing a horn, and singing in a multi-million member Soviet choir, praising the great country we had the unique opportunity to live in. Little did I know that beneath the red flag and patriotic songs, I was unwittingly trudging through the first act of my leadersh!t saga.

Despite my patriotic fervour, my future was not to be that of a proud and committed comrade of the Soviet Union. Life had a different plan for me—one that included a series of personal crises, from the experience of family violence and the unravelling of my marriage to building a life and success in a country on the other side of the world.

Let me take you back to my childhood, where so-called feminine traits were undervalued and dismissed, especially in the work environment. Leading with intuition, kindness, humility and empathy was considered a weakness. This was certainly the case in my family home. I was brought up in a family with a domineering father, a kind mother and two sisters whom I dearly loved. My father's style of parenting was 'Do as I say', not 'Do as I do'. During my childhood and adolescence, I never questioned his style of parenting because it was considered normal. My behaviour, on the other hand, was deemed out of control. As a child, I was labelled 'bossy' and 'overly sensitive'.

Like any Soviet citizen, I was required to be compliant—just another sheep in the herd. I was expected to get an education and then to work hard for little reward. Like everyone else, I would be considered lucky to live in a one- or two-bedroom sh!thole apartment, often shared by multiple generations of one family. Owning a car was considered beyond luxury, so I could not dream even of driving a sh!tbox. Like every other citizen of the USSR, I was obliged to vote at elections with only one candidate on the ballot paper.

I had so many dreams as a young girl and wanted my parents to help and support me to achieve them. But they did not share my aspirations. At the time, there wasn't really any expectation or opportunity for women to succeed in the USSR. My father didn't appreciate my independent and creative spirit, and would often try to crush my dreams. I wanted to be an actress, but he told me that I was not worthy of attending Theatre College. He wanted me to join the police academy instead, because he had connections there and I wouldn't have to sit exams.

My father's misguided attempt to 'help' should have killed my confidence, but, looking back, I now see that his actions led me to grow in confidence and pursue my dreams with passion. Despite his ambitions for me, I went to Theatre College and graduated with a bachelor's degree in musical theatre. I was determined to prove my father wrong and stop him from stealing my dreams. But my independent spirit often felt out of place in the rigid culture of the Soviet Union, where being bossy or overly sensitive were considered flaws rather than strengths. There was no one like Sheryl Sandberg, the former COO of Facebook, who famously said, 'I want every little girl who's told she is bossy to be told instead that she has leadership skills.'

In 1984, at the age of twenty, I had a signed theatre contract and had dreams of shining on stage when an unexpected twist of fate changed the direction of my life. An army cadet, whom I thought embodied a romantic hero straight from the pages of *War and Peace*, swept me off my feet. After a whirlwind three-day courtship, he proposed, and a month later we were married. Instead of basking in the spotlight of theatrical glory, I found myself in an army town far removed from the allure of the stage. There was no theatre in the town, meaning I couldn't work as an actress, and soon I became pregnant. With my husband's scholarship barely keeping us afloat, I had to roll up my sleeves and find a way to put food on the table.

In March 1985 we were back in my hometown, Volgograd, where I welcomed my first daughter into the world. We were ecstatic and named our daughter Valeria, but our little family's bliss was short-lived. We discovered that the place we were renting was sold, which left us homeless and scrambling for a roof over our heads. With nowhere else to turn, we sought refuge with my husband's sister back in the army town. Finding a place of our own to call home wasn't easy, and I also had to find work. After a week of hustling, I landed a gig as a nanny for two little boys. In exchange, we got a tiny room in their apartment—it wasn't much, but it was something.

After my husband graduated, we were shipped off to Dauriya, a blink-and-you'll-miss-it town located in the Russian Far East. Five days on a train with a seven-month-old baby, in a compartment shared with two other people, was a difficult journey and tested the limits of our resilience and adaptability. And when we arrived in Dauriya, it felt like we had landed on another planet. We were far from the comforts of home and family.

As my husband, the hopeful army pilot, dreamed of a bright future, I was slowly accepting the harsh reality that my theatrical dreams might never come true. I also began to realise that my romantic ideas about military men were misguided. I was disillusioned to discover that most of them were just regular guys, and the less brainpower they had the faster they climbed the ranks.

But life goes on. When our daughter turned one, we decided to try for another baby, despite the challenges ahead. I had found a role as an artistic director at the community hall for military officers and their families, which provided some stability and satisfaction amid the turbulence of army life. Yet, the spectre of hardship persisted, casting a shadow over my second pregnancy. Complications, compounded by financial constraints and the absence of proper medical care, created a harsh reality in that far-flung army town.

The nearest proper maternity ward was in a town about 450 kilometres away, so I had no choice but to bring baby number two into the world in the army hospital. It was not a first-class medical facility, to say the least. In the dead of night, amid the chaos that characterises an army hospital,

I faced the daunting prospect of childbirth without adequate medical support. The surgeons were intoxicated by the ghosts of past wars, and probably had more experience drinking than delivering babies. When the moment arrived, it was just me and the midwife against the odds. But despite the chaos and difficulty, I was ecstatic to bring a second daughter into the world.

Julia was born in March 1987, and in December that year life threw me another curveball—a big one this time. My husband's army unit was relocated from Dauriya to Sakhalin Island—one of the largest Russian islands in the Pacific Ocean. But it was not the stereotypical Pacific island with palm trees swaying in a warm breeze and surrounded by a crystal clear blue ocean. Sakhalin Island is north of Japan, and experiences sub-zero temperatures for several months of the year. When we moved, the guys hauled their military gear across land and sea, while the women with kids got the 'luxury' treatment—a charter flight straight to our new 'home sweet home'.

We packed our bags, boarded our flight, and off I went with my two little munchkins. With its rugged beauty and unique position in the Pacific, Sakhalin Island held a sense of mystery and promise. But our arrival was anything but warm and welcoming. We were housed in a building still under construction—no infrastructure, equipment or heat to combat the bone-chilling -30 °C. At least amid the chaos there was a sense of resilience and camaraderie. The hosting crew scrambled some electric heaters and hot plates and we banded together, sharing space and resources with other families and making the best of a challenging situation.

It sounds uncomfortable, and it was. But the struggle didn't stop there. With our men still en route, we had to take matters into our own frostbitten hands and unload our containers of belongings when they showed up a few weeks later. Yep, that's right—DIY moving in the dead of winter, which added to our already chaotic situation.

But the real kicker came early in 1988. That's when the bombshell dropped—my husband was getting shipped to Afghanistan. The Afghan war was a tough time for the Soviet Union. Our government jumped into Afghanistan's mess in 1979, thinking it would be a quick fix, but it turned into a long, brutal fight against Afghan rebels who knew their turf inside out. For soldiers, it was hell—battling in unfamiliar terrain against a fierce enemy. Too many young men never made it back, leaving behind grieving families. It hit hard when I got the news that my husband was headed there, too.

But in the army, orders are like gospel—no one questions them. I was thousands of kilometres away from family and faced the possibility of being a solo parent to two little kids. But I wasn't about to let fear call the shots—I set out to secure my independence. Landing a job as a producer and artistic director at the city of Yuzhno-Sakhalinsk's iconic cultural centre was a win, but the childcare situation threw a wrench in my plans. At age one, Julia was still crawling, and whenever she tried to stand, she'd do it on her tiptoes. The doctors didn't seem worried, saying her development was normal. But I was unable to find proper care for her, and had no choice but to take her to stay with my parents in Volgograd until I could sort things out. When we got to Volgograd, fate dropped another bombshell—Julia was diagnosed with cerebral palsy.

The doctors told me Julia would never walk or talk. The so-called experts were trying to snatch my dream away, but I refused to accept the predictions of these 'dream takers'. Instead, I decided to learn all I could about Julia's condition, and every single day explored innovative technologies and treatments from both Eastern and Western medicine. Today,

Julia is a shining example of resilience. Despite using a wheel-chair most of the time, she can speak and drive a car, and considers herself not as disabled, but as simply living with a disability. She leads a normal life, and her journey continues.

My love for performance kept me going through these challenging times. For a few years, I poured my energy into building my career. I loved my job as a producer and artistic director, and together with some talented peers I launched a popular TV show called *Family Express*. I wore many hats in this production—co-producer, scriptwriter and co-host. Later, we even founded an entertainment company that employed sixty-seven staff. It was a real achievement, especially in a country where most businesses were dominated by men and owned by the state.

But just as it looked like I was finally able to enjoy some happy times, life threw me another curveball. The Soviet Union—the superpower we all knew—began to crumble. Mikhail Gorbachev's reforms, Perestroika and Glasnost, paved the way for political upheaval, and before we knew it the Soviet Union collapsed entirely. It was like the whole world was turned upside down. As wages went unpaid and the nation grappled with its newfound 'freedom', I too struggled to find my footing in a rapidly changing world.

My personal journey also took a dramatic turn just as the Soviet Union itself was undergoing seismic changes. The larger sh!t show was the collapse of a superpower. My personal sh!t show was the unravelling of my marriage. In 1992, I discovered that my husband was unfaithful. This knowledge shattered my world. The decision to divorce was instant, but not without its challenges. In Russian culture, divorced women are often ostracised, and, with two children to support, including one with a disability, the road ahead seemed daunting.

But after my marriage collapsed, I realised that while I was trying to fit in and be like everyone else, I was losing my opportunity to find out how different and incredible I could be. I decided that I needed to be true to myself and control my own destiny, and knew that the only person who could hold me back from achieving my dreams was me. I also made the courageous choice to bring up my two girls alone, determined to instil in them the knowledge that a woman can be strong, and that she should never compromise her own values for someone else.

My courage was rewarded when, just six months after my divorce, I met my current husband, Konstantine—or Kerry, as he is called in Australia. Kerry, a Russian-born Australian, visited Russia on business, and when we met it was love at first sight. He flew back to Australia just a few hours after we met, yet I knew he would come back. And he did— one month later. When he returned to Australia again, he arranged for me to visit him and explore Australia.

During a three-month visit to Australia, I fell in love with Brisbane, the vibrant capital city of Queensland, and its friendly people. It was during that visit that Kerry proposed, and I was faced with another incredibly difficult decision: to follow my heart and leave behind everything I knew, or convince Kerry to move to Russia. Ultimately, he convinced me to move to Australia. It wasn't hard. Australia is known for its spirit of mateship and laid-back lifestyle, and the country's vibrancy and the warmth of its people felt surreal. It was like a dream, and I wanted to pinch myself. I could see endless opportunities for my daughters here, and better access to medical care for Julia.

The decision was made, and in 1994 I moved to Australia permanently. But little did I know—greater challenges lay ahead.

Kangaroos, culture shocks & the KGB

After I accepted Kerry's proposal, I returned to Russia to pack up my kids and my life. But our love story, which should have seamlessly transitioned into a new life in Australia, faced an unforeseen hurdle. Our application for immigration was met with rejection due to Julia's disability. The stark decree was that while Valeria and I could enter, Julia was to be left behind, deemed unwelcome because of her condition. This decision plunged us into an exhausting battle against immigration bureaucracy as we fought to prove that Julia would not be a burden on the welfare system.

Fortunately, a kind officer at the Australian Embassy in Moscow intervened and granted us short-term visitor visas. This allowed us to stay together as a family in Australia and continue our fight from within its borders.

Although I was warmly welcomed into my new country, I could not speak a word of English and greatly missed my family, friends and former career. The fact that Kerry spoke fluent Russian was both a gift and a curse. I could converse easily at home, but being unable to talk to anyone outside my family made me feel isolated. I knew the key to securing my future happiness and independence was to master the language and gain employment, but this was not easy. Conditioned by the restrictions of our temporary visa, which did not allow me to work or study, I started teaching myself English by making lists of fundamental words and phrases. I would then ask Kerry to record them so I could play them back and practise the correct pronunciation. Some days I would ask my husband to drop me off in the Brisbane CBD. There, I was forced to practise my newly acquired English words and phrases. With my husband at work and the children at school, I only had myself to rely on. 'I am just looking around,' was something I said frequently. I felt very vulnerable at these times, which was frightening. I wondered whether I would ever write or speak English fluently.

After this tumultuous period, which involved medical assessments for Julia and bureaucratic struggles, and only two months after our arrival in Australia, we were hit with another blow: Kerry was diagnosed with lung cancer. He underwent surgery and had a third of one lung removed. But incredibly, the diagnosis proved to be false and Kerry's lung tumour was pronounced benign. Nevertheless, this series of challenges left me grappling with feelings of isolation and stress, engulfed by uncertainty and unfamiliarity. The immigration battle, though we emerged victorious, was a harsh lesson in our family's fragility. My husband's health crisis gave me a deep sense of vulnerability, compelling me to vow never to feel so powerless again.

And there were other challenges. Settling into our new Australian life involved far more than adjusting to a new postcode; it challenged every bit of who I was and who I wanted to become. I had landed in a country totally different from the Soviet landscapes I knew, where I was greeted by the peculiar charms of kangaroos, the acquired taste of Vegemite, and an unpredictable twist at every corner. The initial joy of my first visit to Australia was quickly replaced by the realisation that this move wasn't just a geographical leap; it was a plunge into a cultural whirlpool where every norm I knew was flipped on its head.

Life as a new immigrant was challenging. Learning English was critical when it came to fitting in and assimilating. Kids adapt rapidly, which meant that Valeria and Julia quickly became fluent, but I wanted to ensure my daughters maintained their native language amid the predominantly English-speaking environment. Conversations at home often became a delicate dance between English and our native

Russian, with me insisting at times that we maintain our linguistic heritage. This added another layer of complexity to my struggles to find my feet in my new country.

Overcoming the barrier of language wasn't just about learning to communicate; it was about finding my voice in a chorus of unfamiliar accents. After months of English classes, I learned that true fluency demanded more than textbooks and classrooms—it required diving headfirst into the deep end of everyday conversations and cultural nuances. I also realised that, not being a native English speaker, I would never be able to continue my career in the performing arts. So, I had to find a new path. Clutching a dictionary like a lifeline, I enrolled in an office administration course at TAFE.

My time at TAFE provided a true immersion into Australian culture. As I engaged with my supportive and caring classmates, I learned more than just course material. I vividly recall sharing stories about our household chores one day. I proudly mentioned my meticulous ironing routine, which included towels, socks and underwear. My Australian friends were taken aback and gently teased me, explaining that such practices were uncommon in Australia. Determined to adapt and integrate into this new culture, I saw their point and recognised the potential time-saving benefits, especially during the summer swimming season! But old habits die hard. I returned home, and after doing the laundry I hung my clothes on the line, sorted them by colour and smoothed them out perfectly. After they dried, I folded and smoothed them once more before storing them away. Yet, within minutes, I found myself unfolding them, ironing each item meticulously, and then re-storing it. It took months of practice before I finally embraced the more relaxed Australian approach to laundry. This experience taught me a valuable lesson: habits formed early in life are deeply ingrained, and it can be challenging to break free from them, even when they no longer serve us.

Cleaning, and making sure every corner of the house was spotless, was another habit that stemmed from cultural expectations ingrained since childhood. Even a minor oversight would consume my thoughts, detracting from moments of joy and relaxation. One vivid memory that stands out is the visit of my mother-in-law. Despite my meticulous preparations, a small cobweb in the corner of the ceiling overshadowed the entire experience. Instead of enjoying her company, my mind fixated on this imperfection, robbing me of the opportunity to connect and create cherished memories.

During the early days after we received our permanent resident status and due to my limited English proficiency, I could not find work, so I poured my energy into maintaining the house and surrounding land. We lived on acreage, which meant there were always many tasks to attend to—weeding, mowing the grass, trimming trees—you name it. Friends would visit and sometimes mistake me for the gardener amid the constant busyness. It was a distraction, a way to avoid confronting the reality of leaving my home country and everything I knew behind. However, this frenetic activity also prevented me from truly engaging with my new surroundings and embracing the present moment.

The shift from one hemisphere to another had done more than invert the seasons. Despite meeting and mixing with kind and supportive people, questions like 'What's wrong with me?' and 'Will I ever fit in?' became my unwelcome companions, echoing the deep-seated sense of alienation that shadowed my every step. The transition wasn't just about adjusting to a new climate; it was a journey that challenged the core of who I was. Coming from a culture where collective achievements were celebrated and a sense of community was paramount, I felt like a fish out of water in

Australia's individualistic society. While people were friendly and welcoming, I couldn't shake the feeling of longing for my family and friends back home. I missed the tight-knit community I had grown up in, where everyone looked out for each other.

As someone naturally expressive and emotive, communication had always been a vital aspect of my cultural identity. Speaking loudly and using expansive gestures, including hand movements, were the norm in my Russian upbringing. However, upon arriving in Australia, my husband advised me to tone down my use of hand gestures, cautioning that others might perceive it negatively. Unknowingly, this advice instilled a limiting belief within me, leading me to consciously suppress my natural inclination to communicate with my hands.

As a naturally talkative person, the frustration of being unable to communicate or even respond to simple questions weighed heavily on me. Back in Russia, the question 'How are you?' carried significant meaning—it wasn't just a casual greeting; it was an invitation to share one's innermost thoughts and feelings. So, when faced with the same question in my new environment, I couldn't help but feel overwhelmed, believing that people genuinely wanted to know my entire life story. To mask my linguistic struggles, I took up smoking and used the habit as a shield to deter unwanted interactions.

During this challenging period of adaptation and growth, an unexpected opportunity arose that allowed me to enter the family business and marked the beginning of a new chapter in my journey—one filled with its own set of challenges. In 1992, while I was still in Russia, Kerry had made a bold move and bought a company called AIS Water (formerly AIS Enterprises). At the time the business was just a small pool shop tucked away in a suburban shed. It was a humble set-up with only three staff, who mainly sold pool chemicals and did repairs, and sometimes tinkered with small chlorinators.

The original plan was for Kerry to run the business and for me to stay at home to raise my children, learn English and potentially re-establish my performing career. I had a minor role in the company, handling tasks like filing paperwork, sorting out customer accounts, and even putting together some equipment parts. But as time passed, I saw the potential for the business to soar, and I wanted in on the action. I expressed my desire to play a more active role in the company, but was surprised to learn that Kerry was not enthusiastic about this idea. He felt my greater involvement in the business would erode our family life.

There was not much support from the AIS staff either, which I could understand. I was different. I was a foreigner. In fact, because I was Russian, the staff started to call me 'KGB'. But instead of getting upset, I decided to own it. I changed my number plate to 'KGB' and adorned my car's spare tyre cover with the communist symbol from a bottle of Ruski Lemon vodka. Using my new English skills, I told them that the KGB was now official and they should watch their backs.

These tactics created a lot of mirth, and taught me a valuable lesson about the power of humour. This was also the first step in transforming my journey in the Land Down Under from a narrative of disorientation to one of empowerment. Armed with nothing but my resolute spirit and a knack for finding humour in the most unlikely places, I turned each challenge into an opportunity for laughter and learning. Humour wasn't just a coping mechanism; I discovered that it could be a bridge to connection, a universal language that transcended cultural barriers and softened the harsh edges of adjustment.

Laughter became a powerful ally and helped me see the daunting sh!t show of acclimation as a series of comedic episodes. It was hard, but it was a way to turn my struggles into triumphs. In the early days of AIS, I telephoned a customer to remind him about an outstanding account. He told me that he did not understand what I was saying. At home that evening I cried over the incident, but then decided my language limitations would not stand in the way of my success. A few days later, I called the customer back, and, again, he told me he did not understand. I promptly informed him the problem was not my language skills but his inability to listen and suggested he go back to school to learn. After a few minutes of shocked silence, the customer burst out laughing and paid his debt. A few days later, he appeared on AIS's doorstep, wondering who the 'brave girl' was who dared to challenge him on the phone. From that day on, he refused to deal with anyone else in the company.

Each awkward encounter, every cultural faux pas, became a scene in the sitcom of my life, teaching me to embrace the absurdities with a smile. This experience taught me that, sometimes, the best way to claw your way through tumultuous times is to laugh in the face of adversity, to find the lightness in the darkness, and to remember that in every challenge lies an opportunity for growth and joy.

As I continued to immerse myself in my studies, I began applying the newfound knowledge to our family business. I was eager to contribute and make a tangible impact. Despite the challenges of mastering a new language and acclimating to a foreign culture, I found a sense of direction and excitement in this new venture. The lack of support from Kerry and the AIS staff was disheartening, yet it only fuelled my determination to prove my worth and carve out a space for myself within the business.

In these early days at AIS, I noticed that the company enjoyed strong business during the Australian summer, but winter would be quiet. I conceived the idea of a global expansion plan to sell products to the Northern Hemisphere in the Australian winter and trade all year round. However, I realised that AIS would need to develop new products for the global market to do that. Fortunately, Kerry supported this plan, and we decided to reinvest nearly all the company's profits into research and development. Our efforts soon paid off, and, in 1995, AIS sent out its first container of residential chlorinators to Spain. Later that year, the company developed its first commercial chlorinator—one of the many innovations that propelled AIS to the success it is today. It was also a sign that my determination to succeed against the odds was paying off.

Discovering my inner leader

As I delved deeper into both cultural and business spheres, I quickly realised that further education would be my pathway to success. Challenges became my constant companion, but I was determined to overcome them. Reflecting on my education in the Soviet Union, I recalled a robust system that exposed us to a wide array of subjects, from mathematics and chemistry to literature and history. As someone passionate about the arts, I devoted little attention to subjects like mathematics, convincing myself that I was not cut out for them. However, as I found myself navigating the complexities of the business world in my new home, I knew that I needed to expand my skill set. With a fervent ambition to excel in my role within the family business, I made the decision to pursue a Diploma in Business Accounting at TAFE. Yet, my lingering self-doubt regarding mathematical abilities persisted, leading me to postpone tackling the self-paced subject of Business Mathematics until the very end. Despite these doubts, I persevered, ultimately graduating and dismantling one of many limiting beliefs that had held me back.

After completing my studies at TAFE, I made the ambitious decision to further my education by enrolling at the Queensland University of Technology (QUT). Balancing full-time work in the family business with a Bachelor in Business (Accounting) at QUT proved to be a daunting challenge, but I was determined to see it through. This endeavour served as a personal journey of self-discovery and an important part of my integration into my new environment.

Despite my professional growth and further education, assimilation into this strange land continued to challenge me. I had deliberately toned down my expressive gestures, which felt unnatural but seemed necessary. This internal struggle came to a head during a verbal assessment for a subject called Professional Communication and Negotiation. Despite feeling confident in my abilities, I couldn't shake the fear of using too much body language. As a result, I presented in a static manner, sticking to the advice I had been given. However, to my dismay, I discovered that points were deducted from my marks because I hadn't utilised enough body language. This experience marked the first of many calls to authenticity—it taught me that attempting to mould myself into someone I am not only results in setbacks. Embracing my true self, quirks and all, became imperative. It was an early lesson that reinforced the importance of staying true to myself and embracing authenticity, even in challenging situations.

As I went through this personal and professional evolution, I discovered a resilience I hadn't known I possessed. The journey was fraught with moments of doubt and frustration, but each obstacle surmounted brought me closer to a newfound purpose. It was here, amid the trials and triumphs of adaptation, that the seeds of leadership began to sprout, guiding me towards a path where I could not only contribute, but also lead with confidence and compassion. My academic pursuits culminated in graduating from the Australian Institute of Company Directors. Each milestone was both a mark of academic success and a significant step towards establishing my credibility and redefining my role within AIS Water and the wider industry.

In the family business, I faced many challenges. Humour helped break through cultural stereotypes, but gender stereotypes presented another obstacle. When I embarked on a career in the swimming pool industry, I discovered that it was a man's world where men held the reins and women were relegated to the sidelines. It was a landscape dominated by gender biases and entrenched cultural norms, where women were often overlooked and undervalued despite shouldering much of the behind-the-scenes work to keep businesses afloat. In our case, men in the industry would ignore or exclude me from conversations, treating me like an outsider in my own domain. Despite my role in the company and efforts to make a name for myself, I was referred to as 'Kerry's wife'. No matter how hard I worked or how much I achieved, I was always seen through the lens of his success. It was a constant reminder of the uphill battle I faced in asserting my own identity and establishing myself as a force to be reckoned with in the industry. But instead of letting it discourage me, I used it as fuel to drive my determination even further and prove that I was more than just a wife—I was a capable, ambitious businesswoman in my own right.

Drawing on the wisdom of a Russian proverb that says, 'Men are the head, but women are the neck, and they can turn the head any way they want', I was determined to reshape the industry into one where women were seen as equals and valued for their expertise, rather than judged by their gender or appearance. I was also committed to fostering diversity, and spearheaded proactive employment policies that welcomed immigrants, people with disabilities, and mature-age individuals into our workforce. Every obstacle became a stepping stone towards progress as I pushed back against the status quo and fought to carve out my place in the industry.

The difficult decision I had made to educate myself and find a new career paid off, and I eventually assumed the role of CEO of AIS Water. Under my leadership, AIS Water achieved great success, and the initial perceptions of me as the 'crazy Russian woman' were transformed. My husband, colleagues and industry peers began to see beyond the stereotype, recognising the value of my contributions. I surrounded myself with like-minded individuals who shared my values of drive, determination, positivity and innovation.

The value in adversity

My first years in Australia sped by in a whirlwind of change and challenges. But I rose above the labels society imposed on me when I began to question their validity. Was my so-called 'bossiness' not a form of leadership? Was my sensitivity not a form of empathy? This realisation, born through personal and political upheaval, became the cornerstone of my leadership identity. I came to see that my 'bossiness' was indeed a marker of my inherent ability to lead. This chapter of my life underscored a vital lesson: authentic leaders are often shaped by adversity, emerging more resilient and genuine.

My journey might remind you of your own experiences— the ups and downs, the wins, and those unexpected moments that bring joy or a lesson learned. It shows that real leadership comes from facing our challenges head-on and how we deal with them. Consider the adversities you've faced or are currently facing:

- What lessons have these challenges taught you about yourself and the world around you?

- How can you apply the strategies I used in your own life?

- What small step can you take today to transform a setback into a set-up for something greater?

- Reflecting on your past challenges, what unexpected strengths or qualities did you discover within yourself?

- In what ways have your adversities shaped your values and priorities?

- Think about a time when you faced adversity and emerged stronger. What specific actions or mindset shifts helped you navigate that situation?

- How do you maintain a sense of resilience and optimism in the face of setbacks or obstacles?

- How do you strike a balance between persisting through adversity and knowing when to seek help?

As you go through your own journey, remember that every new challenge brings a chance to grow. Approach these situations like an adventure, and be ready to learn and overcome. Let your confidence grow from knowing that you can handle whatever comes your way. As you navigate your own leadersh!t, view each challenge as an opportunity to uncover and refine your unique strengths. Embrace the tumultuous journey of leadership, for it is within these trials that the true essence of your leadership is forged.

CHAPTER 2

MY SH!T SHOW CONTINUES— FROM BURNOUT TO REBIRTH

A S OUR JOURNEY continues, it's time to pull back the curtain on the hidden drama of my adventure. Adapting to a new culture, learning a new language, studying as an adult and embracing my role at our family business were all deeply challenging experiences. I'm glad to say that they were also challenges that I overcame. But there was a high price to pay. In the relentless pursuit of success, I had found myself trapped in a web of stress and health issues.

Growing up in a household where domestic and family violence was the norm, where control was often mistaken for love, and where I constantly heard phrases like 'Do as I say' or 'You're not good enough', instilled in me a deep-seated belief that I wasn't worthy. These experiences shaped my perception of myself, and influenced how I viewed my worth and potential. My failed marriage only reinforced these beliefs, echoing the notion that I was unworthy of love and that someone else was always better than me. So, when I met Kerry, I was determined to prove my worth, to show that I was a good person deserving of love and respect. This led me down a dangerous path of perfectionism.

Moving to a new country added another layer of complexity to my journey. Overnight, I found myself stripped of my established life—familiar surroundings, routines, and even language—and thrust into an unfamiliar world where I had to rebuild a life from scratch. Adapting to a new culture, learning a new language, and navigating a different societal landscape challenged me in ways I had never anticipated. The fact that I made this transition at a mature age meant that certain aspects of my identity remained ingrained, like an accent that would forever mark me as an outsider. The struggle to find my footing in this new reality became all-consuming. With each passing day, I felt the weight of expectation bearing down on me, driving me to prove myself worthy—of love, of opportunity, of recognition. It became a relentless quest to validate my existence, to assert my right to be seen, heard and valued.

The myriad roles I aspired to perfect—wife, mother and friend, business leader and community leader—imposed an immense burden, pushing me to a point where I began to mechanically fulfil responsibilities and neglect my own wellbeing. The stress, initially a psychological strain, began manifesting physically. I had pursued authenticity and perfection in my professional life, but in my personal life I was grappling with weight gain, emotional eating, smoking and sleep deprivation, as well as relying on antidepressants. I had a severely compromised immune system and felt possessed by fear and tiredness. I was in the darkest state of leadersh!t. Every day I felt like I was drowning in the ocean called life, as waves of new challenges tried to knock me down and push me back to where I started.

In 2009 I took on the role of President at the Russian Community Centre, a position that came with a heap of responsibilities. The community hall I inherited was on the brink of bankruptcy, with an old building in need of renovation and membership in decline. Despite already feeling exhausted, I was determined to turn things around and transform this struggling centre into a thriving hub—a home away from home for Russian-speaking immigrants and the wider multicultural community.

I put together a board of individuals who shared my passion for diversity and uniting the community for the greater good, and together we worked tirelessly and achieved remarkable results. We gave the hall a much-needed facelift and installed disability access. We organised a series of successful cultural events that boosted our finances and brought the community together. Our hard work paid off, attracting attention from volunteers, community members, and even politicians who generously supported our initiatives.

It was a proud moment for me as I stood on stage during one of our events, singing and watching my team in action. But amid the success, I started to feel like I was losing balance. Everything seemed to blur, and I felt disconnected—like I was merely an observer rather than a participant. The next day, I fell ill, but it was more than just a physical ailment—I was struggling mentally. It was a wake-up call that I couldn't ignore. The intense pressure of running multiple businesses, managing family life, and fulfilling my duties as a mother had taken its toll. It was clear that something needed to change before it spiralled into tragedy.

At the age of fifty I had been teetering atop a precarious stack of chairs. The chairs bore various labels: 'mum', 'wife', 'CEO', 'friend', 'community leader' and more. I had been juggling all of these responsibilities in a kind of bizarre circus act. This wasn't ordinary multitasking; it was an extreme sport of emotional endurance. My circus act might have looked clever from the outside, but here's the thing about juggling—sometimes you end up dropping more balls than you can keep in the air. Inevitably, it had happened. The crash. My role at the community centre brought down that stack of chairs and my juggling act was over. It wasn't a gentle tap on the shoulder; it felt like a cosmic sledgehammer bringing me to a screeching halt. I wasn't just tired. I was like a comet that had blazed through the sky and burnt itself out.

The path to healing

The path to healing began when a friend intervened, and emphasised the temporary nature of the relief provided by the antidepressants I was taking, and urged me to re-evaluate my life for true happiness. This marked the beginning of my awakening, which was further catalysed by a transformative retreat in Phuket. I went to the retreat with some of my dear friends, and it became a sanctuary for renewal and self-discovery. My friends' support was my lifeline, pulling me from the depths of despair towards a path of rejuvenation.

Falling ill was a harsh wake-up call, a stark reminder that I could no longer sustain the pace of my life, and the retreat experience was instrumental in reshaping my approach to stress and wellbeing. During those two transformative weeks, I shed not only physical weight but also the heavy burdens of emotional pain. I discovered the profound connection between diet and wellbeing, and made a solemn commitment to prioritise my health above all else. Immersed in practices of yoga, meditation and mindfulness, I discovered the power of healing energy and the amplifying effect of group meditation. The retreat was about more than detoxing my body; it marked the beginning of a soul-searching odyssey and a quest to heal the deep-seated traumas that had accumulated since childhood. Gradually, the vibrant essence of my true self began to resurface, breathing new life into my weary spirit. This period of holistic healing peeled away years of burden, leaving me rejuvenated, with a mind free from fog and a heart ready to embrace leadership with clarity and purpose.

This journey taught me a fundamental truth about leadership and self-care: the importance of securing your own oxygen mask first. It's a metaphor that resonated deeply, underscoring the need to nurture oneself to effectively lead others. This realisation became my guiding principle, allowing me to find balance, to rejuvenate, and to stand strong as the best version of myself, continually evolving and embracing the journey of self-improvement. I also learned a crucial lesson about stress: its impact lies not in its presence, but in our response to it. I began to view stress as a potential ally, a source of energy that, when channelled correctly, could drive me forward. Research supports this dual-edged nature of stress, suggesting that while a positive outlook can enhance motivation and performance, prolonged stress without relief can be detrimental to health.[1]

During subsequent visits to similar retreats I delved even deeper into the recesses of my soul. Confronting childhood fears and untangling the knots of resentment towards my father were daunting tasks, but ones that I tackled head-on. It was during this time that I was introduced to Pranic Healing and 'The Work' of Byron Katie, two modalities that would become integral to my healing journey.

Pranic Healing offered me a path to self-discovery, introducing me to the transformative power of Meditation on Twin Hearts developed by Master Choa Kok Sui. Through this practice, I discovered the profound truth that we receive in giving—a principle that would guide me on my journey

---

1   Lazarus, R. S., & Folkman, S. (1984). *Stress, Appraisal, and Coping.* p. 31.

back to wholeness and becoming a better person and a better leader.

The teaching of Byron Katie offered further illumination, challenging me to question my perceptions and beliefs. Through her work, I came to understand that our reality is shaped not by external circumstances but by our reaction to them—our perception. Through the lens of 'Loving What Is', I began to see each obstacle as an invitation for personal growth and every setback as a pathway to more profound insight.

This shift in perspective liberated me from the constraints of victimhood and empowered me to take ownership of my own happiness and wellbeing. I realised that everything unfolds for me, not against me—an empowering revelation that would forever reshape my life.

Leading with the heart

As the flames of burnout receded, I began to craft a different style of leadership, one stitched with threads of empathy, vulnerability, and a rare kind of love—unconditional and all-encompassing. Transitioning from a conventional leader to a spiritual entrepreneur attuned to intuition and soulful guidance, I embraced a new ethos: leading with the heart. Gone were the days of prioritising spreadsheets and strategies above all else. Instead, I sought to infuse every decision and interaction with soulful intention. Recognising that at our core, we are all human beings with passions, fears and dreams, I sought to nurture not only profits but spirits.

This transformation began with a shift in my belief system, rooted in the childhood notion of prioritising others above self. I learned that extending kindness and respect to others starts with practising self-love and self-respect. Cultivating a mindset of gratitude and positivity became a daily ritual, as I embraced morning meditation and affirmations to set the tone for the day ahead. The practice of Twin Hearts meditation proved instrumental in opening my heart and crown chakras, allowing healing energy to flow through me and into the world.

With this spiritual practice as my compass, I found myself becoming more attuned to the energy of those around me, intuitively understanding their needs and emotions. Leading with empathy and humanity became an integral part of my identity. No longer could I view my role as simply instructing others on what to do. Instead, I recognised each individual as both a name on a payroll and a unique soul under my care. They deserved guidance, support and a compassionate ear whenever needed. In this journey, they became my teachers as much as I was theirs.

Embracing vulnerability as a leader was initially challenging. I held on to the belief that true strength lay in stoicism and unwavering resolve. However, a pivotal moment shattered this misconception when I unexpectedly broke down in tears before my team. Contrary to my fears of losing respect, I was met with an outpouring of support and solidarity, revealing the strength in vulnerability and the power of authentic leadership.

Since then, I've fostered a culture of transparency and trust by openly sharing both my triumphs and challenges with my team. Rather than isolating myself in my office, I actively engage with my staff, whether it's joining them for lunch, taking short walks, or having informal chats after hours. Building and nurturing trust has become my foremost priority, rooted in my personal journey of overcoming adversity and embracing the transformative power of authentic leadership. This metamorphosis was not just about healing myself; it was about setting a precedent. It was about showing that in both business and life, vulnerability can be a superpower, empathy a tool for connection, and love the ultimate guiding principle.

As CEO of AIS Water, I poured my heart, my creativity and my hard-earned insights into the business. Leadership for me transcended conventional boundaries; it was about kindling a fire of innovation and passion, about steering the ship with a clear vision and a steady hand. As the company expanded and became increasingly successful, my influence grew. I received invitations to join industry boards, where I passionately advocated for diversity and gender equality, and fostered collaboration among manufacturing businesses.

Fast forward several years, and AIS Water has become a highly respected company, boasting over fifty national and international awards for innovation, best business practices and leadership. Among our notable achievements was developing a groundbreaking lower salinity chlorine generator designed for public swimming pools. Our innovative technology emerged from our steadfast commitment to overcoming the challenges presented by traditional chlorine dosing methods. While effective in disinfecting pools, these methods often carry adverse health implications for swimmers and environmental risks, particularly concerning our precious resource—water. Perhaps most notably, our chlorine generator significantly reduced water consumption.

As the company continued to go from strength to strength, we decided to embark on our first strategic expansion plan, and set our sights on North America—a market sixty times larger than Australia. This expansion required us to undertake a complex approval and certification process and, just as we were making progress with this, the COVID-19 pandemic brought the world to a standstill. As an essential business, we remained in production, but the challenges presented tested our resilience and the core of our business philosophy.

We gathered in the car park every morning for our daily staff meetings. The faces before me bore the weight of anxiety and uncertainty, seeking reassurance during turmoil. It was a humbling experience, and the responsibility of guiding my team through unprecedented times lay heavy on my shoulders. As the days turned into weeks and the weeks into months, the pandemic began to take its toll on us all. The relentless pace of work left me feeling drained and exhausted, desperate for even a moment of respite. Yet, I clung to the belief that the universe would never burden us with more than we could bear. Turning to meditation and nature walks for solace, I sought refuge in these quiet moments of reflection and found renewed strength to face the challenges ahead. I reminded myself and my team that adversity only serves to reveal our true strength and resilience.

After navigating through the challenges of the pandemic, we shifted our focus inward, recognising that our most valuable asset was our people. Drawing from my experiences of moving countries, mastering a new language, stepping into leadership and overcoming adversities, I became passionate about opening doors of opportunity for everyone in our organisation. We want each team member to love coming to work and feel that their ideas are valued and that they belong. Belonging is one of our core values, and it's something we all crave in life. My role as a leader is to ignite the leadership spark in every team member, inviting them to join the dance because we all know it takes two to tango. By prioritising a positive work environment and fostering a sense of community among like-minded individuals, we cultivated a workplace where everyone felt valued, supported, and empowered to pursue their true calling.

Transforming stress from a crippling force into a catalyst for positive change was a journey of profound self-reflection and adaptation. It required a deep dive into my intuition and business acumen, but I gradually steered our family business towards new heights of success. This transformation not only altered perceptions within AIS Water and the broader industry, but also marked a significant evolution in my own identity.

The power of reflection

As I reflect on my relentless pursuit of success and the high price I paid for it, I can't help but acknowledge the deep-rooted causes behind my drive to perfect every role in my life. I firmly believe that our upbringing and childhood traumas shape us in profound ways, often leading us to carry unresolved wounds that continue to haunt us. These wounds linger in our subconscious, shaping our beliefs and behaviours until we confront them head-on.

I found that creating times, and techniques, when I could calmly reflect on my journey helped me grow. As we continue to peel back layers and unmask harsh realities, remember that reflection isn't about dwelling on the past; it's about using it as a launchpad for what's next. It's also essential to recognise that transformation doesn't happen overnight or through mere dreams. When you realise that something in your life needs adjustment—whether it's your feelings, actions or circumstances—you must be prepared to put in the effort to turn your newfound insights into forward momentum.

So, here is the toolkit that helped me turn my reflections into a superpower. These are the tools and exercises that worked for me, and I wholeheartedly invite you to explore them and embark on your own journey of reflection and personal growth.

The mirror monologue challenge: Stand before a mirror and unleash your own uncensored story. Talk about your fears, dreams, and the sometimes comical reality of life. This is your stage, your script, and your moment to shine.

My experience: *Facing my reflection was like confronting a character in a play—raw, unscripted and real. It was more than a chat; it was a deep dive into the heart of my experiences.*

The journal jamboree: Create your own journal jamboree. Fill it with the spectrum of your experiences—the good, the bad and the downright funny. Let your words paint the picture of your unique journey.

My experience: *My journal became a carnival of thoughts, a chaotic yet beautiful mess of highs and lows, triumphs and trials.*

The 'what if' game: Ask yourself, 'What if?' Imagine a world without fear. Write down these fearless dreams. Remember, it's about dreaming big and unchained.

My experience: *I swam through my fears, surfacing with dreams that were no longer chained by doubt.*

Comfort zone jailbreak: Identify something outside your comfort zone and take the plunge. It's about expanding your horizons and discovering new facets of yourself.

My experience: *I stepped out of the mundane, embracing the thrill of the unknown, from striking up conversations with strangers to embracing new challenges.*

Quest for brutal honesty: Engage in conversations seeking brutally honest feedback. Embrace the discomfort, for it's in these moments that real growth happens.

My experience: *Seeking unfiltered feedback was my ticket to growth—every truth, no matter how hard, was a step towards personal development.*

Change is a gradual process, and there is no one-size-fits-all solution. What worked for me may not work for everyone, and that's perfectly okay. We all have our unique approaches and needs. What matters is finding what serves you best and propels you towards a better version of yourself.

CHAPTER 3

ANOTHER SH!T SHOW— RISING FROM THE ASHES

OW, LET'S SHINE the spotlight on a remarkable chapter in this journey, featuring my friend, Lisa Lockland-Bell. Picture this: she was originally meant to be my accent coach, but life has a way of surprising us with its plot twists. Lisa became so much more than that. She stepped into the roles of vocal coach, confidante, and my 'partner in crime' on life's rollercoaster ride. Our bond is a testament to the magic that happens when paths cross at the right moment and create strong friendships.

Our journey together, filled with moments of growth and spiritual exploration, blossomed amid our shared struggles and triumphs. I believe life is like tuning into a radio frequency. As we evolve, embrace self-development, and open our hearts to empathy and love, we start to align with higher vibrations. On this frequency, we meet souls like Lisa— those who have been waiting, ready to join us on the same radio band.

Lisa's story deeply resonated with me, echoing the resilience and indomitable spirit that resides within us all. Her life is a narrative of transforming setbacks into stepping stones, a journey of using life's challenges as the raw materials to build her ship of dreams. It's a poignant reminder that adversity isn't just a hurdle; it's a launchpad to greater heights, a catalyst that propels us towards our true destiny.

In her own unapologetically honest and raw style, Lisa will share her journey. It's a story of navigating through life's tumult, of finding her North Star, and emerging as a beacon of light and inspiration for others. So, without further ado, let's welcome Lisa Lockland-Bell to our narrative stage. Brace yourself for a tale of strength, courage, and the transformative power of embracing life's curveballs.

LISA'S STORY

There was a time when I couldn't say the word 'sh!t', let alone fathom the thought that my own sh!t could stink. After all, I was an 'opera singer darling'. My head was so far off the ground, all I could smell was the rose petals being strewn on the stage as I daydreamed about being idealised by my adoring fans.

If only I knew then what I know now—that a good sh!t tells a thousand tales about who you are, and I'm not just talking about the smell.

I am talking about the wealth of information my sh!t was saying without me knowing it.

The lack of frequency, the erratic shape, loose consistency, dark colour and foul odour were screaming that my life, and my sh!t, was, for want of a better word, completely and literally in the sh!t.

In 2002, as a twenty-two-year-old, I was diagnosed with stage three Hodgkin disease, and endured six months of the strongest chemo they could give me plus six weeks of radiotherapy. You would assume that I may have learned about my health. But nope, not me. Apparently, I still liked the feeling of wallowing in my sh!t.

At least that's what it felt like as I sat on my hospital bed, convalescing (playing the victim) after a radical hysterectomy for my second cancer diagnosis. This time, it was stage four cancer of the cervix. In walked my OB-GYN, oncologist and surgeon. Now, as you probably know, to get one specialist into a hospital room is a small miracle, but to have all three was sobering (I was going to say complete sh!t, but enough now).

The awkward silence was deafening as they stared at the collage my children had made to keep me company while I was in the hospital. Finally, they said, 'Lisa, the good news is the pathology results are clear and we are ninety-five per cent sure we have got it! BUT we want to be 105 per cent sure, so we are going to give you six weeks of radiotherapy because here is the bad news ... you cannot get this disease again. You're only thirty-four years of age, and your body will not respond to any more treatment. There is nothing more we can do for you.'

There it was; the angels sang and cherubs were flying as my 'aha' moment struck me to the core. For the first time since I was a little eight-year-old girl, an unbridled energy stirred from within, fearlessly rising to the surface. In that moment, I surrendered, moving beyond my very horizontal mindset, vertically deep diving back into my truth. And just like we tune into the frequency of a radio station, I tuned into my gut voice. At full volume, I felt the deafening cries screaming, 'Get up and out of your sh!t; You will do whatever it takes to survive! Your children are only two-and-a-half and four, and you will not leave them for someone else to raise. Clearly, something you are doing IS NOT WORKING, and you need to take responsibility for yourself once and for all!'

I instinctively knew that to survive, the situation called for a sustainable environment within my mind, body and spirit. But I was also confused. I had come from a space of not believing in myself, and yet I was secure in knowing a part of myself (that I hadn't met before) in such a way that I was confident enough to move forward. I was driven to meet and get intimate with this enigma that was bounding freely within. The question was, 'How?' Well, you're about to find out.

While setting my intentions, I had to focus on changing everything that wasn't in alignment with my higher purpose, values and desires. This required a few short, sharp decisions to ensure I got to where I wanted to be. I was desperate for a team of experts that understood my enquiry to learn how to live, not just survive!

For anyone who has gone down the path of self-discovery, you know full well that having a team of people to lean on is essential.

The other thing I realised was that I am easily distracted, so I decided to keep myself accountable for the whole journey.

This is how I went about it...

Phase one started with Reiki, a Japanese form of alternative medicine known as energy healing. It was an introduction that catapulted me onto the fabulous adventure known as alternative healing. While my new world was directed with wonder and excitement, I'm not going to sugar-coat any part of the journey because this transformation was incredibly tough and at times terrifying.

As I left behind the people who didn't understand why my life was going down this path, the sense of loneliness was overwhelming. In fact, the words 'You do you, and I'll do me' were often repeated at the end of a family battle as I tried just one more time to explain why I was becoming that 'weirdo hippy' in the family. This fitted in perfectly with my 5am commitment to yoga and meditation. Taking the time, making space, being still and listening allowed me to show up and connect to the intuitive decisions that now permeated my sphere of consciousness. All that my family saw was someone they once knew sitting and humming in the light of a candle, repeatedly muttering mantras to herself.

This ability to tap into my intuition was my dormant superpower. That enigma that I mentioned earlier was secretly relieved that I was going through so much physical pain, because now I was listening and ready to recalibrate my internal navigation system—with the destination coordinates set on nirvana.

When I reflect on what drove me to push through the pain, keep up with my exercise, ask millions of questions, put on my makeup to face the world, and drink horrible green juices, the answer is simple. I wanted to experience life without prejudice.

How did my life become so sh!t?

You are right if you're thinking there is a part of the story I haven't shared yet. How did I get here?

I grew up with a father who suffered from bipolar disorder. Back in 1984, it was called a nervous breakdown or manic depression.

For twelve years, I lived with a Jekyll and Hyde character. One moment I was the apple of my father's eye, and the next I was the bane of his existence. Today you would see it as a form of domestic violence; I lived in a hostile environment that caused me to combat a constant state of fight or flight.

Within that environment, my cognitive development was impacted, leaving me with a set of behavioural conditions designed to survive this environment. Being vulnerable or just being a girl (let alone someone who was creative) was seen as weak in my father's eyes; dramatic and totally irrelevant. So, being the empathetic and obedient daughter, I believed I was a bad person; Dad wouldn't lie to me, right? The only option for me was to shut down. Try to become someone else, turn off my senses, and the most harmful thing of all—stop trusting my gut. In other words, place my sense of self in a coma. While this worked to help me survive back then, you already know the long-term results of this survival strategy.

So, to answer the original question of what drove me... I was desperate to know what happiness felt like again. I wanted to experience that core need of human connection. As a toddler, I was nurtured by and connected to both my grandfathers, so I remembered what it was like to feel loved and understood. But as life took over and Dad got sick, I became angry at everything and everyone. This is when, I believe, the DIS-EASE started to manifest in my body.

It was true that I was not being heard or understood, but what I didn't understand was the reason why.

I was not listening to myself! I was so conditioned to care about what the world thought of me that I had completely ignored the silent, ever-present witness: myself.

Stop lying to yourself

You might feel uncomfortable with phase two of this story; I know I did. If a healing guru like Deepak Chopra were to ask you: 'When are you going to stop lying to yourself?', what would you say? I am not talking about the big lies that are going to sabotage someone else's life. I am talking about the little lies that are killing you softly. Things like 'one more wine doesn't matter' or 'judging someone can't hurt' or 'life is not worth living without eating meat'.

This was my challenge. Starting with one hour at a time, I was not allowed to lie to myself about anything. Not even the words that the 'scumbag voice' in my head was screaming. Phrases like 'you're not good enough' or 'you don't deserve that job'. I had to flip everything and ask, 'Is this the truth?' Try it. I can guarantee that much of the time you are lying to yourself. This was the turning point to my survival. The practice is beautifully outlined in *The Four Agreements* by Don Miguel Ruiz and Janet Mills.

Here comes nirvana

I remember when ayurvedic medicine became the bedrock of my world. After over thirty-five years of carrying weight, dealing with hormone imbalances and wrangling a fiery temperament, this is where I learned that my sh!t was, in fact, one of the greatest moderators to how I was digesting my life. As I eliminated meat, cheese, wheat, tomatoes and wine from my diet, my blood work improved and the inflammation in my body decreased.

The first sign of change was, you guessed it, in my poop. It wasn't so rancid, and neither was I. It was a strong and structured form, and so was I. It was consistent, on time, and satisfying, and so was I. Could it be that my life was no longer in the sh!t? Well, I wasn't there yet, but I was certainly on my way.

Something started to shift in my mind as my new world filled with possibilities. I'll never forget when I noticed that not only was I seeing colours differently, but the contour of my eye had relaxed and changed shape as well. I was totally smitten with my transformation, and it no longer made sense for me to do things that I knew didn't serve me. Why would I choose to eat foods that I know will create an acidic environment that could kill me? Why would I surround myself with toxic environments and people if they weren't in alignment with my goals? At first, the outcomes were subtle, but, with consistent practice, simple.

Ayurvedic treatments, remedies, food, vitamin support and lifestyle changes. I became obsessed with the challenge of rejuvenating and teaching my system how to walk, breathe and digest life once and for all.

The next step

It takes focus, dedication and a strong will to do something that you haven't been raised to believe and does not come naturally. To help you understand, from an ayurvedic perspective, my body type (dosha) is Pitta, which means I run hot. I'm a passionate Aries who loves to be in complete control, micromanaging the bejesus out of everything and everyone. So, this whole 'woo-woo hippy' concept of letting go left me feeling vulnerable and terrified.

There were times of tears and tantrums, and I was often exhausted from building my new life, but to give up was to die. The concept of giving up never even crossed my mind, and I kept investing in my personal development. One thing that helped me transition to a higher level of consciousness was *The Law of Attraction*, a book by Esther and Jerry Hicks. With Oprah Winfrey's words in my head, I had begun to 'live my best life' by creating my own reality. The theory behind this must-read is that we create our own realities. Not only do we attract things we want, but we also attract things we don't want.

We attract the people, the stuff in our homes, and the money in our bank accounts through our thoughts and feelings.

By this stage in my development, I was already practising detachment and was less likely to be defined by external stuff. This didn't leave a lot of room for the Bentley I was driving from the mansion on the weekdays or the helicopter we flew to the farm on the weekend. Six years into my transformation, these things didn't make me a better human anymore. In fact, they were actively pulling me in the opposite direction, leaving me exhausted as I tried to adjust my new self to make others happy.

It's not easy to open up and tell the world that I walked away from a life that most people would dream of. After all, I had been through so much illness. Why couldn't I just stay in this dysfunctional marriage? Believe me, there were many sideways looks of 'She's crazy!'

The four soul questions

'She's crazy' could not have been further from the truth. I had a clear mind, strong body, and, best of all, perfect poop. This was my moment to take a leap of faith and practise everything that I had learned.

With my four soul questions in tow, I finally let go of the oars, started to flow, and accepted all that the universe had to offer me.

Led only by my intuition and daily practice of asking my four soul questions, I felt safe and supported, knowing that as long as I was in alignment with this practice, the universe would provide the answers. And it did.

1 Who am I?
2 What do I want?
3 What is my purpose?
4 What am I grateful for today?

The past eight years have seen my two worlds integrate and grow into a thriving business. I took the physical voice, the skill that I had spent the previous twenty-five years studying and practising as a professional opera singer, and the internal voice, the very thing that had kept me alive, and created a program to help others think, speak and breathe truth into their life.

As a two-time cancer survivor, ACCF Ambassador, vocal coach, and mother of grown children, I know that there are thousands of women in the world who have unspoken words stuck in their heart. They hold on to their truth, shy away from telling their narrative, and sidestep the opportunity to reach their ultimate potential.

I know the suffocation of having words stuck in your heart, but also the sheer ecstasy of releasing those words and living your truth.

The Performance Studios now includes a globally renowned network of award-winning artists and speakers who live their truth every single day.

To postpone an early curtain call, I implore you to acknowledge your sh!t, set your voice free, and live your truth.

LISA LOCKLAND-BELL, Founder, Chief Executive Officer, Principal Vocal Coach, Performance Studios Australia

After hearing Lisa's powerful story, it's clear that life's greatest challenges often serve as the most profound teachers. Her journey, much like the ones we all embark on, is riddled with obstacles, but it's her response to these obstacles that defines her path. Just as Lisa found strength in adversity, each of us has the capacity to transform our own challenges into opportunities for growth.

Her story is a reminder that our struggles are universal, yet uniquely personal. Whether it's facing a health crisis, navigating personal upheavals, or reinventing ourselves, the essence of our journey is the same—it's about rising from the ashes, stronger and more resilient.

A practical approach to setbacks

Now that we've delved into Lisa's inspiring journey and the insights gained from her experiences, it's time to explore some practical strategies. Both Lisa and I employed specific approaches to navigate our toughest times, and these strategies can be invaluable tools for turning your setbacks into set-ups for future success. Here are some actionable steps to guide you on your own path of transformation:

Embrace self-reflection: Moments of crisis can serve as opportunities for deep introspection. Ask yourself tough questions and be honest with your answers.

Prioritise self-care: Focus on your physical and mental well-being. Simple practices like meditation, yoga or journaling can provide a solid foundation for healing and growth.

Seek support: Don't hesitate to reach out for help. Surround yourself with people who uplift and support you, just as Lisa and I did for each other.

Adopt a growth mindset: View every challenge as a chance to learn and evolve. Embrace the mindset that every experience, good or bad, is a step towards personal development.

Take small, consistent steps: Progress is often a series of small actions rather than giant leaps. Celebrate every small victory on your path to recovery and transformation.

Use these suggestions as a starting point for your journey of transformation. Remember, every challenge holds the seed of an equal or greater opportunity.

CHAPTER 4

LEADING A SHIFT—
STRATEGIES FOR CHANGE

N OW LET'S MOVE on from the stories of my and other people's sh!t shows and their transformations, and begin to turn inward. How will you transform your own sh!t show? How will you begin to lead a shift in your own life? As you have learned from my story and Lisa's story, it is not easy to turn the ship of your life around. But it can be done.

In this chapter, we're ready for something new. We're moving on from just getting through tough times to really taking charge and making positive changes. We'll dive into how we can lead with purpose and make a real difference, using everything we've learned from our toughest times.

So, let's take a deep breath, feel proud, and get excited for what's next. We're not just dealing with challenges; we're actively shaping our future. Let's celebrate this journey we're on. Each step we take is a step towards becoming better, stronger and more purposeful. And that's something worth celebrating.

In this chapter, I am going to give you thirteen practical strategies for change. These are the tools I've gathered along my path, from the bustling streets of the Soviet Union to the vibrant landscapes of Australia. Each strategy is a piece of wisdom, tested and proved in the fires of personal and professional challenges.

Strategy 1: Understanding the current state—facing your truth

The journey of transformation begins with self-awareness. It's about looking at yourself honestly and acknowledging where you are. This process isn't always comfortable, but it's crucial. It's like standing in front of a mirror that reflects not just your appearance, but your inner state, your fears and your potential.

When I first arrived in Australia, I faced a stark reality check. The move involved more than adapting to a new country; it was about adapting to a new version of myself. I had to confront some hard truths about my skills and approaches, and acknowledge that what worked back home wasn't sufficient here. This was my moment of facing my truth.

How to conduct your own reality check

Set aside some quiet time for introspection. Use a journal to reflect on where you are in your life. Be brutally honest with yourself about areas where you're succeeding and where you feel stuck or lost. Remember, this isn't about self-criticism; it's about laying the groundwork for meaningful change. Consider questions like: What am I avoiding? What changes am I resisting? What are my current challenges?

Strategy 2: The power of affirmations— becoming, not faking it

Affirmations are not just words; they are declarations of our inner strength and capabilities. They help us shift our focus from our limitations to our potential. When we consistently affirm our strengths and aspirations, we start to embody these qualities, leading to tangible changes in our lives and mindset.

Adapting to my new life in Australia was a challenge filled with moments of disappointment, homesickness, and a deep sense of disconnection. No matter how hard I tried, satisfaction and comfort seemed elusive. Then, during one particularly trying day, I found myself repeating a simple but powerful mantra: 'I can do it. I am strong. I am resilient.' This became my daily chant, a source of solace and empowerment.

Over time, these affirmations evolved to match my needs. Whenever I felt a lack of self-love, I would remind myself, 'I am my number one customer and client.' This practice of positive affirmation slowly transformed my outlook. I began to notice a shift in my attitude and perspective, leading to positive changes in my life. Today, affirmations are an integral part of my morning routine, setting the tone and intentions for my day.

How to integrate affirmations into daily life

To make affirmations work for you, integrate them into your daily routine. Choose phrases that resonate with your goals and repeat them every morning. Whether it's for self-confidence, resilience or success, let these affirmations be your first thoughts each day. Remember, it's not about simply saying the words; it's about believing in them and allowing them to shape your reality.

Take a moment to reflect on the qualities you want to foster or the goals you aim to achieve. Craft affirmations that align with these aspirations. Make them personal and positive, and express them in the present tense. Regularly repeating these affirmations will gradually shift your mindset, empowering you to become the version of yourself you aspire to be.

*Sample affirmations can be found in Appendix 2.

Strategy 3: Goal setting with intent— working backwards to move forward

This strategy is about the power of commitment as a catalyst for personal and professional development. By committing to a challenging goal, you are compelled to find solutions, learn new skills and seek support. It's a proactive approach that turns potential obstacles into opportunities for growth.

When I first stepped into the manufacturing world, I felt as out of place as if I had arrived at a formal gala in a superhero costume. To integrate and excel, I adopted a strategy of pushing myself out of my comfort zone. I would set ambitious goals or volunteer for challenges that seemed slightly beyond my reach. Whether it was speaking at an industry conference or volunteering for a community project that stretched my abilities, I committed first and figured out the 'how' later. Once I had committed, I sought help from my team of experts who could help me rise to the occasion. This method wasn't just about achieving the goal at hand; it was about upskilling myself, strengthening my capabilities and building invaluable connections. Commitment to the final outcome became my key to growth.

How to set bold goals and achieve them

When faced with a new opportunity, don't shy away, thinking you're not ready. Instead, commit to the goal and then work backwards to figure out how to achieve it. This mindset will push you to learn quickly and adapt, turning challenges into stepping stones for success.

Reflect on an area in your life where you want to see improvement. It might be a skill, a professional competency, or a personal trait. Set a goal in this area that seems slightly beyond your current reach. Once you've committed to this goal, identify the steps and resources needed to achieve it. Embrace the learning process as you progress towards your goal and watch how this commitment transforms you.

Strategy 4: Embracing a growth mindset— challenges as hidden opportunities

This strategy is the essence of a growth mindset—seeing challenges not as dead ends, but as pathways to new heights. With this mindset, each challenge becomes a puzzle to solve, a lesson to learn, and a chance to expand your capabilities. It will shift your perspective from one of avoidance to one of engagement and curiosity.

In my journey, every new challenge felt like receiving an invitation to a party where I knew no one. I often envied people who seemed to have an easy, obstacle-free path, while my own journey felt like a relentless series of hurdles. It was a constant battle of adapting, learning and, sometimes, feeling like I was treading water. But with time, I began to see these challenges in a different light. They weren't just obstacles; they were hidden opportunities, each with the potential to lift me to the next level. Instead of dreading them, I learned to embrace them, to feel a sense of excitement and anticipation for the growth they would bring.

How to change your challenge narrative

Start viewing challenges as opportunities for personal and professional growth. When faced with a new challenge, instead of asking, 'Why me?', ask, 'What can I learn from this?' or 'How can this make me stronger?' Change your internal narrative to see each challenge as a step towards becoming a more resilient and skilled individual.

Reflect on a recent challenge you faced. Instead of seeing it as a setback, try to identify the opportunities it presented for learning and growth. What skills did you acquire or sharpen as a result? How did it contribute to your personal or professional development? Embrace this mindset for future challenges and watch how they transform into valuable growth experiences.

Strategy 5: The art of visualisation— crafting your tomorrow

Visualisation is a powerful tool that goes beyond mere wishful thinking. It involves mentally constructing a detailed image of your desired outcome, making it as realistic as possible. This practice is not only about seeing the end goal, but also about instilling a deep sense of belief and commitment to achieving it.

My journey with visualisation started with an inspiring tale from the book *Chicken Soup for the Soul*. I began to practise picturing my goals vividly in my mind, transforming them from mere thoughts into tangible visions. This wasn't just daydreaming; it was a deliberate effort to shape my future. As I improved, my visualisations began to manifest into reality.

Visualisation evolved into my tool for bringing dreams to life, turning abstract ideas into concrete achievements.

As I mastered visualisation, I introduced it to my team. We would describe what success looked like for our projects and then affirm it by saying, 'Done.' This practice became more than goal setting; it was a collective visualisation of success, a shared belief in our ability to achieve our objectives.

How to visualise

Start by creating a vision board or a mental movie of what you want to achieve. Fill it with images, words and scenarios that represent your goals. Regularly spend time visualising these goals, immersing yourself in the feelings of achievement and success. This process helps to align your subconscious mind with your conscious efforts, turning your visions into reality.

Reflect on a goal or aspiration you have. Visualise achieving it in great detail—what does it look like, feel like, and sound like? Now, mentally, or aloud, stamp it with the word 'Done', reinforcing your commitment and belief in its realisation. Practise this visualisation regularly and observe how it transforms your approach and attitude towards your goals.

Strategy 6: Cultivating a supportive environment—dream builders and challengers

Finding a balanced, supportive environment is crucial. It's a blend of nurturing cheerleaders and honest challengers. This mix encourages progress and provides reassurance, while also driving you to push your boundaries and realise your full potential.

Reflecting on my past, I realise how my father, in his own way, was an unintentional dream taker. His approach, rooted in tough love, unknowingly fortified my resilience. This early lesson was crucial when I first arrived in Australia, where I faced a new world without a network of supporters or dream builders. I had to navigate through a maze of dream takers, who, despite good intentions, often hindered rather than helped.

Over time, I recognised the power of surrounding myself with the right people—those who not only believe in my dreams, but also challenge me effectively. Today, my network consists of dream builders who encourage and affirm, as well as constructive challengers who push me to question and excel. This balanced environment has become a key element of my journey, offering both a safety net and a launchpad for growth.

How to build a supportive network

Take a moment to reflect on your personal and professional network. Identify the dream builders, the challengers and the dream takers. Consider how each of these influences shape your journey.

Who are the people who truly support your aspirations (dream builders) and those who constructively challenge you (challengers)? Actively seek and nurture these relationships. They are not just your cheerleaders but also your coaches, guiding and pushing you towards your goals. Now ask: Who are the dream takers? Think about ways to tactfully manage or limit interactions with dream takers.

Strategy 7: Continuous learning— the journey through books and beyond

Education is never 'done'. You're never too old to learn, and lifelong learning should be the focus for every leader who wants to escape their sh!t show and lead a shift in their lives and their leadership.

Books have been my steadfast companions in life, guiding me through the tumultuous journey from the USSR to Australia. In my youth, they were sanctuaries, offering refuge to a sensitive soul in a world that often felt confining. As I embarked on my new life in Australia, books continued to be a source of solace and learning.

Throughout my journey, books have been more than just sources of information; they have been beacons guiding me through life's challenges. Combined with formal education and the relentless pursuit of new skills, this continuous learning has been my pathway to transformation—from a hesitant immigrant to a confident leader.

How to embrace lifelong learning

Don't limit your learning to just books or classrooms. Life itself is a classroom. Embrace a holistic approach that includes real-life experiences, observation and formal education. Each book you read, each new skill you acquire, and every challenge you overcome is a step towards personal and professional growth.

Reflect on how learning has shaped your journey. Are there new areas of knowledge you can explore to further your growth? How can you integrate a balanced mix of book learning and real-life experiences to enrich your understanding of the world and yourself? Remember, every page turned and every new experience is a step towards a more enlightened you.

Strategy 8: Time management mastery— juggling priorities without dropping the ball

Time management isn't just about efficiently organising tasks; it's about prioritising your wellbeing. It's easy to fall into the trap of trying to please everyone and putting yourself last. But true time management mastery comes from recognising that your health and wellbeing are paramount. Without this foundation, everything else crumbles.

There was a point in my life when navigating through complex roles felt like performing a high-wire circus act. I was constantly juggling responsibilities as a mother, wife, CEO, friend, community leader ... the list goes on. But in my attempt to keep every ball in the air, I neglected the most crucial element: myself. This oversight led to a severe burnout, a state where I was overwhelmed, unhealthy and functioning like a zombie. It was a wake-up call that highlighted the crucial role of effective time management and prioritising self-care.

How to manage time well

Start by creating a balanced and realistic schedule. Allocate time wisely for each role you play, including non-negotiable 'me time'. Stick to this plan rigorously. Bending these rules can quickly spiral into old habits and chaos. Remember, managing time effectively means managing your life holistically.

Reflect on how you currently manage your time. Are there areas where you're neglecting your needs? Think of ways you can restructure your day to prioritise your health and wellbeing. Effective time management means not only completing tasks, but also ensuring you're in the best shape to perform them. It's about recognising that you can't help others effectively if you're running on empty.

Strategy 9: Asking for help— strength in vulnerability

Asking for help is an underrated skill. It's not a sign of weakness, but a testament to strength and wisdom. It shows a readiness to learn and a willingness to grow. By asking for help, we open ourselves to new perspectives and solutions we might not have considered otherwise.

In my early Australian days, grappling with a new language and culture, I learned the critical importance of seeking help. It wasn't just about language; it was about survival in a new world. I would often find myself in the city, armed with an address and my basic English skills, asking strangers for directions. Their willingness to assist, often going out of their way to help, was both heart-warming and eye-opening.

How to be open to asking and receiving

Never hesitate to seek guidance or clarification. Embrace your vulnerabilities as opportunities for growth and connection. Asking for help can lead to unexpected friendships, insights and lessons. It's about shedding the armour of self-sufficiency and embracing the collaborative spirit of mutual growth.

Consider a current challenge or goal where you might benefit from external help or guidance. Who in your network or beyond could provide this assistance? Reflect on any hesitations you have about asking for help and the potential positive outcomes of reaching out. How can embracing the act of seeking help strengthen your journey and open new doors of opportunity and collaboration?

Strategy 10: Embodying resilience— stronger muscles, greater resilience

What doesn't break you makes you stronger. Challenges are opportunities to exercise and strengthen our resilience muscles. Just like physical exercise, resilience is built through consistent practice. Over time, our ability to handle stress and bounce back from setbacks becomes stronger and more effortless.

At AIS Water, I was often seen through a lens of stereotypes and misconceptions. The label 'KGB', initially a jab at my Russian heritage and language struggles, became a metaphor for the numerous challenges I faced. I transformed it into a symbol of resilience, humorously embracing the label by displaying it on my car's number plate. This act of playful defiance was a turning point, a way of declaring that I wouldn't be defined or diminished by others' perceptions.

My journey was about more than just a label. It was a continuous process of facing and overcoming perceptions— being an immigrant, a woman in a traditionally male industry, and dealing with the 'pretty face, no brain' stereotype. Each of these challenges presented an opportunity to prove my worth, to demonstrate that resilience isn't just about enduring but about transforming adversity into strength. I learned that while we can't always change reality, we can choose how we react to it. By meeting scepticism with grace, humour and determination, I turned doubters into supporters and transformed perceived disadvantages into assets.

How to cultivate resilience
Embrace tough situations as a gym for your character, where every obstacle is a weight to lift, making you stronger and more adaptable. Remember, resilience also involves self-compassion; knowing when to push forward and when

to pause for self-care is crucial. Make a habit of stepping into uncomfortable zones, while also being mindful of your wellbeing.

Reflect on a recent challenge you faced. How did you handle it? Did you see it as a setback or as an opportunity to grow stronger? Consider how approaching future challenges as opportunities to build resilience can shift your perspective and enhance your ability to cope. What aspects of your reaction could be improved to foster a more resilient mindset? Think about specific strategies you might use in future situations to enhance your resilience. Journaling these reflections can help you recognise patterns in your responses and guide you towards more resilient behaviours.

Strategy 11: Embracing humour— lightening life's load

Humour is more than just a way to entertain; it's a powerful tool for making ourselves approachable and relatable. It helps in smoothing over awkward situations and turning potential embarrassments into endearing moments.

When I first arrived in Australia, humour became my unexpected ally. I quickly discovered the power of laughter to break down barriers and forge connections. Public speaking was initially daunting, especially with my thick Russian accent and imperfect English. But I turned this into an advantage with a bit of self-deprecating humour. At events, I'd quip, 'Some of you might struggle to catch every word I say, but you'll definitely remember the Russian who's always "rushing around"!' This always lightened the mood in the room, and helped me connect with my audience on a more personal level.

How to harness the humour within

Don't be afraid to use humour, especially when facing challenging situations. It can be a great way to ease tension, create rapport, and make your interactions memorable. A good laugh can also be a great stress reliever, both for you and those around you.

Reflect on a recent situation where things didn't go as planned or you faced a challenge. How could humour have changed the dynamics of that situation? Think of ways you could use light-hearted self-deprecation or humour to ease tension and connect with others in similar scenarios in future. Consider how embracing humour can transform not just your perspective, but also the atmosphere around you.

Strategy 12: The power of silence— more than just quiet

Scientific research, such as the study published in *Heart* magazine in 2006, has shown that just two minutes of silence can be more calming than listening to soothing music. Another fascinating study in 2013 demonstrated that silence could even foster new brain cell growth in mice.[2] These findings underscore that silence is more than just a lack of noise; it's a powerful tool for mindfulness and personal growth.

When I started going on silent retreats, I discovered that the greatest challenge wasn't not being able to speak, but quieting the internal chatter that relentlessly played in my mind. Silence opened my eyes to the unnecessary volume of words we use daily and the barrage of thoughts that occupy

---

2   https://www.ncbi.nlm.nih.gov/pmc/articles/PMC4087081/

our minds. It was a profound realisation that sometimes, in saying less, we can hear more.

However, silence has its flip side. Misused, it can lead to misunderstandings or even conflict. Think about times when a 'joke' was taken the wrong way, or gossip led to unintended consequences. Silence teaches us restraint, helping us to choose our words wisely and avoid causing harm unintentionally. It's a balance between speaking up when necessary and embracing quiet when it's beneficial.

How to practise mindful silence

Begin by incorporating short periods of silence into your daily routine. Use this time to be fully present, observing your surroundings and your thoughts without judgement. This practice isn't about suppressing your personality; it's about enhancing your awareness and control over your reactions and responses. Whether you're an introvert or an extrovert, silence can be a valuable skill to cultivate.

Reflect on how silence, or the lack of it, impacts your daily life. Consider times when speaking less could have led to a better outcome, or moments when embracing silence brought clarity and calm. How can you incorporate mindful silence into your daily routine to enhance your communication, relationships and personal growth?

Strategy 13: Practising forgiveness— the path to liberation

Forgiveness can release you from the burden of carrying resentment, anger or bitterness towards another person or people. When you forgive, you let go of the negative emotions that tie you to the past, allowing you to move forward and live more fully in the present. It's not always easy, but the benefits it brings to your mental, emotional and even physical health make it a powerful and transformative practice.

My journey to embracing forgiveness began amid the trials of my daughter's health issues and the initial hardships of adjusting to life in Australia. In those challenging times, anger and blame were my instinctive responses. However, I gradually realised the uselessness and harm of holding on to these negative emotions. It was a profound realisation that every challenge also offered a lesson. This shift in perspective became more profound during a trip to Bali, where I learned to incorporate forgiveness and gratitude into my daily routine. This practice wasn't just about letting go of negative feelings; it was about transforming my approach to life's difficulties into one of understanding and empathy.

The practice of forgiveness taught me an invaluable lesson: liberation. Forgiving others, the world around me and, crucially, forgiving myself, lifted a weight off my shoulders. It enabled me to view situations from a perspective of growth rather than resentment. This shift didn't happen overnight, but it gradually instilled a sense of peace and understanding within me, allowing me to navigate life's challenges with a more balanced and empathetic outlook.

How to create a forgiveness ritual

Start by setting aside a few minutes each morning to engage in a forgiveness ritual. Begin by forgiving those who may have wronged you, whether intentionally or not. Extend this forgiveness to the world for any frustrations it may bring that day and, importantly, forgive yourself for any mistakes you might make. In the evening, reflect on your day. Visualise how you could have approached situations differently, avoiding hurt or anger, and then repeat the forgiveness ceremony. This consistent practice will gradually embed a deeper sense of empathy and understanding in your daily life.

Reflect on a recent situation where you felt wronged or frustrated. How did you react? Now, imagine approaching the same situation with forgiveness and understanding. How might this change your perspective and response? Consider how integrating a daily practice of forgiveness could transform not only how you react to challenges, but also how you view yourself and others. Journaling these reflections can be a powerful tool for recognising and solidifying this transformative approach.

As we conclude this chapter on 'leading a shift', let's reflect on the significance of these strategies. Each strategy is a step not just towards change, but towards a deeper understanding and mastery of our own narratives. Embrace this part of the journey with the humour and heart it deserves. Remember, change is not solely a destination to reach but a path of rich experiences, learning and growth. It's about appreciating every challenge and victory, and the countless possibilities they unveil.

Let's move forward with excitement for the lessons ahead, armed with resilience and the joy of discovering our best selves in every twist and turn of this adventure.

CHAPTER 5

LEADING A SHIP—
GIVING BACK

TRUE LEADERSHIP is not just about achieving personal and professional success, but also about the positive impact we can make in the broader community. The next part of our journey will explore how extending our influence to give back can create a lasting legacy and a more fulfilling leadership experience. In the journey of leadership, the act of giving back transcends the conventional boundaries of success, embodying the essence of true influence and impact.

Surviving the personal and professional difficulties I encountered in the Soviet Union, moving to Australia, and overcoming the language barrier, gender biases, a career change and a spectacular burnout are all achievements to be proud of. But perhaps my proudest achievements are those that have been bestowed upon me for my work as a community leader.

My journey in Australia began under the banner of survival. Each endeavour, from mastering a new language to navigating the complexities of business leadership in a so-called male dominated industry, was a step towards proving my worth. In this relentless pursuit, the idea of celebrating my achievements seemed almost indulgent, and was overshadowed by the next looming challenge.

So in 2005, I was taken aback when I received a nomination for the Telstra Business Women's Awards. The nomination was made by friends who saw potential in me that I had yet to appreciate. I was even more astonished when I was recognised as a state finalist for this prestigious award. That moment became a pivot that shifted my perspective. It illuminated the idea that my journey, perceived through my eyes as mere survival, could be a beacon of inspiration for a diverse audience. The confines of my self-imposed limitations were shattered; it was as if a window had been thrown open after years of darkness. Suddenly, the world appeared in vivid colour, teeming with possibilities and opportunities previously obscured from view. I knew I had to find the courage to speak up.

Initially I had reservations about speaking at the awards night, but after delivering my speech I was astonished when one of the previous national award winners candidly remarked, 'You bitch! I wish I had your accent; it would set me apart.' Her bold comment not only elicited laughter, but also helped me embrace my unique identity and the distinctiveness it brought to my journey. From that moment, I was ready to use my voice, and my nomination for the award unlocked a series of opportunities to share my story, transforming platforms into stages where my narrative could inspire and resonate with others.

Leadership beyond the boardroom

At the heart of my commitment to giving back is a deeply personal campaign against domestic violence, which is rooted in my own life story. My father, a figure who inter-twined mentorship with pain, left an indelible mark on my life. My mother, just eighteen when she married, had no per-sonal power and was denied agency in decision-making. My father's anger-fuelled, drunken outbursts were a recurring horror of our family life. Every blow inflicted on my mother reverberated within me, and as a child I keenly felt her pain. It's a pain that seared itself into my identity, fuelling a deep-seated resolve to end such atrocities.

In May 2018, my father's passing marked a transforma-tive moment. As life ebbed from his body, the dominant monster of the past gave way to a man craving love and for-giveness. His final words, expressing love and pride, revealed the lost little boy within him—one who yearned for affection, yet failed to grasp that violence is never synonymous with love or respect. In witnessing his final moments, I saw not just the man who had caused such pain but also the scared child he once was. This moment of profound clarity tran-scended personal grief and sparked a realisation about the pervasive cycle of violence that affects so many families. It became my mission to not only heal my own wounds but to prevent others from experiencing similar pain.

My father's transformation served as a poignant reminder of the importance of forgiveness and compassion. It fuels my commitment to using my voice to ensure women suffering from domestic violence know they're not alone and that help is available. Through initiatives like Dancing CEOs, I've raised awareness and funds for organisations like Women's Legal Service Queensland, providing crucial support to survivors.

My message has not always been well received. An emo-tional moment that stands out occurred during a political debate, when I confronted an audience initially resistant to my message. I began with a declaration: 'Hello, my name is Elena Gosse, and I say no to domestic and family violence.'

In response I faced the boos and jeers from a largely intoxicated, unsympathetic crowd.

But as I unveiled my story, the boos and jeers died away and the room became enveloped in a heavy silence, the kind that precedes a profound change in perspective. I shared my experiences of growing up amid violence, the complex emotions I felt towards my father, and the life-altering realisations at his deathbed. My unfiltered truth resonated, transforming jeers into reflective silence and scepticism into support. Perhaps they had expected me to play the blame game—but I never do that. I believe all problems are related to childhood trauma and unfortunately sometimes we, as women, must take some responsibility. I believe we will achieve much more by lovingly guiding perpetrators towards opening up and healing, and allowing them to be part of the solution to heal the world.

This experience underscores the impact of sharing one's story. It wasn't just an act of courage; it was a catalyst for change. The raw truth of my story had the power to peel away layers of prejudice and apathy, touching the hearts of listeners in profound ways. In numerous instances, presenting to predominantly male audiences, my story has evoked a wide array of emotions—from tears to silent departures, from reflective silence to heartfelt conversations. It became evident that this work, particularly with those who have perpetrated violence, is not just necessary but crucial. The ability to change perceptions, to lift the weight off hearts and souls, and to inspire action, reaffirms the necessity of vulnerability and honesty in our collective fight against domestic violence.

Domestic violence doesn't discriminate; it affects people of all ages, colours, sexual orientations and professions. We must change the values we impart to future generations, encouraging men to embrace their emotions and seek help before resorting to violence. Sharing my experience has sparked meaningful conversations and connected me with fellow survivors and reforming perpetrators, reinforcing the power of our collective voice.

My advocacy work is driven by the belief that domestic violence is not merely a private issue, but a societal scourge that demands a collective response. By sharing the story of my family, I seek to shed light on the hidden agony of countless individuals and advocate for a future where children grow up in environments of understanding and openness, rather than fear and aggression.

Closely related to my fight against domestic violence is my mission to empower women. This dedication stems from a deep-seated belief in women's potential and the transformative power of self-determination. Far too often, I've witnessed women sacrificing their happiness and dreams to serve others, only to be sidelined and unfulfilled. The pressure to portray a perfect life on social media perpetuates a harmful illusion, exacerbating feelings of inadequacy and leading to mental health struggles and substance abuse.

Empowering women to take control of their destinies, build confidence, and unleash their voices is a driving force in my life. My journey serves as evidence that any barriers can be transcended with the right attitude, determination and support. I reject the notion of 'faking it till you make it', and opt to stay true to myself and embrace my authenticity. Confidence is the ability to turn thoughts into actions, enabling us to navigate risks and pursue our aspirations without hesitation. A key aspect of building confidence is focusing on what we love.

Women possess the education, experience and drive to lead effectively, yet often need a well-defined voice that reflects their expertise and values. We must find and use our voices, as they have the power to effect meaningful change and shape the future of our communities and societies. As we navigate these unprecedented times, embracing our femininity and cultivating empathy and inclusivity in our leadership is vital. Our voices have the potential to break barriers, foster understanding and drive positive transformation. Speaking out and using words that challenge the status quo can pave the way for a more equitable and compassionate world.

Leadership from within the boardroom

From within the boardroom, I champion another cause close to my heart. Water, our most precious resource, is often overlooked in its significance to our lives. Yet, just like a living being, water deserves to be treated with love, respect and gratitude. It possesses a unique power to change its state and form, serving as the life force within us. Our bodies comprise sixty per cent water, our brains seventy-three per cent, and our lungs eighty-three per cent. Water is vital for our wellbeing.

My journey into water conservation began with a startling realisation: the staggering wastage occurring within swimming pools. Millions of litres of water are lost to evaporation, backwashing filtration systems and continuous refilling every year, with public pools being the most significant contributors. This highlights the urgent need for sustainable solutions.

But the problem goes beyond mere wastage. The chemicals used to sanitise pool water, such as chlorine and algicides, threaten groundwater if not properly managed. Runoff issues stemming from improper pool maintenance exacerbate contamination, further jeopardising our ecosystem.

In response to these challenges, the team at AIS Water has pioneered innovative technology that revolutionises water treatment in swimming pools. By safely producing chlorine onsite and inline from minerals and salts dissolved in pool water, ranging from the lowest salinity up to seawater, our technology not only meets stringent FINA standards but can save an astounding 1.6 million litres of water in a single fifty-metre swimming pool. This game-changing approach enhances the swimming experience and demonstrates our unwavering commitment to sustainability.

Driven by our passion for innovative solutions to combat water wastage in swimming pools caused by outdated chlorine dosing methods, I have become a sought-after speaker at industry conferences, advocating for adopting environmentally conscious technologies. With every opportunity, I strive to raise awareness about the importance of water conservation and inspire others to join us in protecting our most precious resource—water.

These are just a few of the ways I have embraced my leadersh!t journey by turning the ship of my life around and finding a way to use my leadership position to give back to the community—to lead a ship—both from within and outside the boardroom. Instead of being a barrier, each challenge I have encountered has become an opportunity for growth and enlightenment. Through adversity, I have emerged as an authority, equipped with the wisdom and compassion to guide others through their own trials and tribulations. My purpose is clear: to enhance lives by sharing my stories and helping those in need. With each narrative shared and each hand offered in assistance, I move closer to fulfilling my calling and making a tangible difference in the lives of others.

My commitment to living life to its fullest has drawn me towards experiences and people that have not only supported my growth, but have also been enriched by our interactions. It is this cycle of mutual growth and empowerment that underpins the essence of giving back in leadership.

Every small victory celebrated, every challenge overcome, adds depth to our narrative, making our leadership journey not just a path we walk, but a story we share. It's in the act of sharing these stories that we extend our influence, encouraging vulnerability, empathy and resilience in others. By championing success and advocating for open dialogue, we foster an environment where growth and learning are communal experiences.

My nomination for the Telstra Business Women's Awards was a turning point in my life. It helped me find my voice and heralded a cascade of recognitions that painted a broader picture of my journey. Over fifty national and international accolades have since graced my path, each a testament to various facets of my leadership and commitment to technological and societal advancement. From being celebrated as Best Manufacturing Executive to being honoured as Business Person of the Year, these accolades underscore the impact of my endeavours across the professional and community spectrum.

The journey of acknowledgement has extended beyond professional circles, with recognitions like the Fundraising Champion, Westfield Local Hero and the QUT Outstanding Alumni, highlighting the wider resonance of my contributions. The reach of my influence was further amplified through a TED Talk, which connected with over a million viewers, echoing the universal themes of empowerment and finding one's voice. Leading AIS Water through the ebbs and flows of industry challenges, from the global financial crisis to the unprecedented trials of a pandemic, contributed to a narrative of resilience and innovation. The culmination of these efforts and recognitions was symbolised by the Order of Australia medal, a prestigious acknowledgement that encapsulated the essence of my professional and community contributions.

But true leadership manifests itself in numerous ways beyond business accolades—through mentorship, advocacy and storytelling. My role as a public speaker and mentor transcends the imparting of knowledge; it's about igniting change, inspiring courage and nurturing the next generation of leaders. By sharing our vulnerabilities and strengths, we light the way for others, making leadership a journey of collective elevation.

I continue to happily lend my voice to those who need it most. Whether through my keynotes like 'Finding Your Voice', 'Leading like a Woman' or my new keynote, 'Leaders Enhance Life', I'm passionate about giving back. Seeing the impact these messages have on my audiences is incredibly fulfilling. In every crowd, there are individuals who resonate deeply with the insights I share.

This book, too, is a form of giving back. It's a platform to reach even more people, offering them inspiration, guidance, and a sense of connection. Through its pages, I want to touch lives, spark meaningful conversations, and empower others to find their voices and lead with purpose. It's my way of contributing to a world where every voice is heard and valued.

Each of us possesses a unique voice, a tool with the potential to effect profound change. By using our voices, we not only transform ourselves but also the lives of others.

How to give back

As we draw this chapter to a close, we stand on the face of an essential realisation: leadership is not a destination, but a continuous journey. The act of giving back, a cornerstone of true leadership, is not just about the impact we make on others but also about the profound enrichment it brings to our own lives.

In giving back, we share not only our resources, but also our vulnerabilities, our triumphs and our lessons learned. This exchange fosters a deeper connection with our own values and humanity, providing fresh perspectives and insights that fuel our personal and professional evolution. It's in this cycle of giving and receiving, teaching and learning, that we find the essence of sustainable leadership.

There are many ways to give back—here are some suggestions you may like to consider:

Mentorship: Offer your expertise and insights to guide others. Whether in formal settings or casual conversations, your story might be something someone needs to hear right now that will give them hope and point them in the right direction.

Community engagement: Actively participate in causes close to your heart. Your contribution can amplify efforts in areas like domestic violence prevention, empowering women, or any cause that resonates with your values.

Empowerment through education: Engage in initiatives that educate and empower, particularly in areas where misinformation or stigma prevails. Your voice can be a powerful tool for awareness and change.

Future letter writing: Write a letter to your future self, outlining your hopes, goals, and the lessons you want to remember from the stories you've read. This can serve as a powerful reminder of your journey and aspirations.

Community engagement plan: Come up with a concrete plan to give back to your community, inspired by the stories of contribution and change. This could involve volunteering, starting a community project or simply performing acts of kindness.

Personal story sharing: Share your own stories of overcoming challenges, practising vulnerability, or giving back with a trusted friend or family member. Authentic stories and raw unfiltered truth have the power to connect, inspire and foster a sense of shared humanity.

As we transition to the next chapter, 'The Continuous Cycle', let's carry forward the understanding that our leadership journey is perpetually renewed through each act of contribution, each story shared and each life touched. This ongoing cycle of growth, grounded in the principle of giving back, ensures that we remain not just leaders in title but in action and spirit, continuously evolving and adapting in our relentless pursuit of making a meaningful difference in the world.

CHAPTER 6

LEADING A SHIP—
THE CONTINUOUS CYCLE

ELCOME TO the final chapter in our journey. Here we discover that the show never ends. Our odyssey through our own sh!t shows, through leading a shift and through leading a ship, culminates in the knowledge that we are on a spiral journey of evolution. Our voyage is eternal and our growth perpetual.

This chapter is an expansion of our journey, offering further exploration into continuous growth. Here we embrace new challenges with curiosity, committing to lifelong learning and evolution. It's an invitation to climb the staircase of our personal and professional lives, with each step elevating us towards our highest potential.

Change: A constant companion

Embracing evolution is recognising change as our constant companion. In both life and leadership, the only true constant is change. It is the universe's oldest trick—an unexpected guest arrives and rearranges the furniture of our lives, but often brings with them new vitality and perspective. This realisation challenges us to view change not as an adversary to be resisted, but as an essential catalyst for our growth and progress.

Change is deeply integrated in who we are, compelling us to venture beyond our current limitations and explore new territories. It's akin to updating our personal software; while we remain the same at the core, we continuously enhance ourselves, fixing bugs and adding new features. This ongoing process of self-improvement isn't aimed at reaching a definitive end goal but is about embracing a lifestyle of perpetual growth and adaptation, making the journey of self-improvement an integral part of our daily existence.

Understanding change goes beyond acknowledging it as an external force that disrupts our routines; it's an internal drive that propels us towards embracing new possibilities and shedding our former selves for growth and fresh experiences. Every instance of change invites us into the unknown, urging us to get comfortable with leaving our comfort zones. This is where true leadership is forged—not in the safety of the known, but in the unpredictable and often challenging realms of new opportunities.

As we embrace the continuous cycle, change transforms from a mere disruption to a powerful driving force for our growth. It constantly pushes us from the comfortable ground of our present selves into the expansive sea of possibilities within us. With each wave of change, we are presented with opportunities to expand our horizons, explore uncharted paths and redefine our capabilities.

Learning: A lifelong endeavour

At the heart of our continuous cycle lies the endless spiral of learning. Think of this journey as climbing a grand spiral staircase, where each step represents a unique learning opportunity. Some steps might be steep, requiring effort and perseverance, while others could be slippery, challenging our balance. There are those steps so inviting and comfortable that they tempt us to linger, basking in the satisfaction of our achievements. But the staircase calls us to climb higher, promising an ever-expanding horizon of knowledge and experience with each ascent.

This perpetual motion of learning mirrors the natural cycles around us—the changing seasons, the phases of the Moon, the ebb and flow of tides. Each cycle brings renewal and growth, teaching us that repetition is not mere redundancy, but an opportunity to layer new insights over the foundations of old ones.

In this never-ending spiral, every challenge we face, every mistake we make, and every victory we celebrate becomes a lesson. These lessons are the building blocks of wisdom, the kind that can only be gained through lived experience. They remind us that to stop learning is to stagnate, to remain fixed while the world, in its constant state of flux, moves on without us.

Yet, the beauty of this cycle is in its accessibility. It doesn't require grand gestures or monumental challenges to engage. The spiral turns with the small, everyday decisions we make, the questions we ask, the curiosity we nurture. It's in the books we read, the conversations we have, and the quiet moments of reflection we allow ourselves.

This cycle emphasises the collective nature of our journey. We are not lonely travellers, but part of a vast network of learners. Every interaction is a chance to teach and be taught, to share our spirals with others and intertwine them, creating a richer, more complex tapestry of knowledge and understanding.

As we continue through the continuous cycle, embracing the endless spiral of learning is crucial. Each step not only broadens our knowledge but also enriches us with wisdom and character depth, placing growth at the core of our evolution. This journey, deeply personal yet interconnected with others, invites us to strive for the best versions of ourselves. Amid this ascent, it's all too easy to become engrossed in the climb, forgetting to pause, breathe and appreciate the scenery. The intensity of our focus can sometimes overshadow the joy of the journey.

Humour: Learning to laugh

Integrating humour into our evolutionary journey lightens our load. It allows us to chuckle at our missteps, delight in surprises, and remember not to take ourselves too seriously. Consider humour as the shock absorber on our bumpy road to growth. It smooths out the ride, making it more enjoyable. Without a laugh at our attempts to master new skills or understand ourselves better, we miss out on the joy of self-improvement.

Research underscores the value of humour in our lives. A study in the journal *Psychological Science* found that humour not only relieves stress but can enhance problem-solving abilities by broadening our perspective.[3] This ability to see

---

3   Ruby T. Nadler, Rahel Rabi, John Paul Minda. 'Better Mood and Better Performance: Learning Rule Described Categories Is Enhanced by Positive Mood'. *Psychological Science*, 2010; 21: 1770-1776 DOI: 10.1177/0956797610387441

the bigger picture can be invaluable as we tackle the complexities of personal and professional development.

It's often said that laughter is the best medicine, and there is truth in this. Laughter triggers the release of endorphins, the body's natural feel-good chemicals. According to the Mayo Clinic, laughter also increases oxygen intake, stimulates the heart, lungs and muscles, and increases the endorphins released by your brain. This cascade of physical benefits accompanies the mental clarity and emotional resilience that humour fosters, making it an indispensable tool in our continuous cycle of learning and growth.

Humour also connects us. A study from the University of North Carolina found that shared laughter promotes bonding and increases group cohesion. This sense of connection is vital as we navigate the spirals of learning and evolution, reminding us that our journey is shared, not solitary.[4]

The value of a good laugh is clear. It does more than just brighten the journey; it strengthens resilience, sparks creativity and fosters connections. Integrating humour into our evolutionary path lightens each step and makes obstacles feel less daunting, all while building a sense of community and joy.

Reflection: Looking back to move forward

Reflecting on our experiences, both the highs and the lows, allows us to understand how far we've come and where we might head next. It's about pausing in our ascent up the spiral staircase of learning to look back, appreciate the view, and gather insights for the climb ahead.

---

4   Laura E. Kurtz, Sara B. Algoe. 'When Sharing a Laugh Means Sharing More: Testing the Role of Shared Laughter on Short-Term Interpersonal Consequences'. *Journal of Nonverbal Behavior* | Issue 1/2017.

Reflection acts like a rear-view mirror. Just as a driver glances back to understand their vehicle's position relative to the road, reflection allows us to consider our past experiences, not with regret or nostalgia, but with a sense of appreciation and insight. This process of looking back is crucial for moving forward with purpose and clarity.

Reflection is not just about dwelling on the past; it's a strategic pause, a deliberate slowing down to take stock of our experiences. It's akin to an artist stepping back from their canvas, allowing them to see the broader picture and decide where the next brush stroke should land. This perspective is invaluable as it informs our future decisions, ensuring that our actions are guided by the wisdom gained from our past.

This reflective practice can be as simple as a quiet moment of contemplation at the end of the day, a journal entry that captures our thoughts and feelings, or a deep conversation with a trusted friend or mentor. Each act of reflection serves as a point of synthesis, where our experiences are distilled into actionable insights.

Additionally, reflection fosters a sense of gratitude. By looking back, we can't help but feel thankful for the journey, for the people we've met along the way, and for the lessons that have propelled us forward. This gratitude enriches our journey, adding a layer of depth and meaning to our continuous cycle of learning and growth.

Reflection offers a way to celebrate progress, assimilate lessons from past experiences, and navigate the future with clarity and purpose. This process of looking back enriches our understanding, transforming reflection from mere reminiscence into a strategic guide for future endeavours. It ensures that each forward step is deliberate and in harmony with our growth.

Support: Surrounding ourselves with dream builders

Picture this: as you climb each step on the spiral staircase of personal and professional growth, the voices of support around you blend like a well-orchestrated symphony. These voices belong to the people who see the potential within you, even when you might doubt it yourself. They're the mentors who share their wisdom, the peers who offer their insights, the friends who lend their unwavering support, and the family members who provide unconditional love. They are your dream builders.

Catalysts in our lives are like the conductors of this symphony, guiding us through the complex compositions of our growth. They have a unique ability to ignite a spark within us, pushing us to shed the layers that no longer serve us and embrace the possibilities that lie ahead. With a gentle nudge or a thought-provoking challenge, they help us maintain our focus and direction, ensuring we don't lose sight of our goals amid life's distractions.

Dream builders, on the other hand, are the composers of our aspirations. They help us craft the vision of what we aim to achieve, turning the melodies of our dreams into tangible realities. Through their support and belief in our capabilities, they reinforce the notion that our aspirations are valid and attainable, providing the motivation needed to keep going.

The beauty of this symphony of support lies not only in the strength it provides, but also in the vulnerability it nurtures. In moments of doubt or setback, these individuals remind us that it's okay to falter, that every misstep is part of the learning process. They embody the empathy and understanding that make the journey bearable, but also deeply human and relatable.

Furthermore, this symphony is not a one-sided affair. As much as we benefit from the support of our catalysts and dream builders, we also play a similar role in the lives of others. In sharing our own experiences, victories and lessons learned, we contribute to the harmony of their journeys, making the climb a collective endeavour where everyone's growth is celebrated.

Adaptability: Becoming masters of change

Adaptability is an essential skill that enables us to overcome life's inevitable changes. The ability to adapt allows us to pivot gracefully when faced with unexpected challenges and to view every twist as a new path to explore. It's similar to jazz improvisation, in which musicians veer off the written score to create something spontaneous and beautiful. In the same manner, we must be open to improvising, to adapting our strategies and outlooks in response to life's unpredictable rhythms.

Research underscores the value of adaptability. A study published in the *Journal of Vocational Behavior* highlights that adaptability correlates positively with career satisfaction and overall wellbeing.[5] Adaptability enables individuals to navigate the complexities of changing environments with resilience, turning potential stressors into opportunities for personal and professional development.

In every chapter of my journey, adaptability has been the cornerstone of my resilience. Embracing a new country, mastering a new language, and acclimating to a novel

---

5   Ryan D. Duffy, Richard P. Douglass, Kelsey L. Autin. 'Career adaptability and academic satisfaction: Examining work volition and self efficacy as mediators'. *Journal of Vocational Behavior* Volume 90, October 2015, pp. 46-54.

culture laid the foundation for a lifetime of transformative shifts. Leading AIS Water through turbulent times and championing domestic violence prevention have further underscored the critical role of adaptability. These experiences have ingrained in me the power of flexibility in overcoming obstacles. Each challenge has taught me to view life's hurdles as invaluable opportunities for growth, learning and evolution.

To master the art of change, we must cultivate an open mindset, one that welcomes new experiences and perspectives with enthusiasm rather than apprehension. This mindset is about flexibility, resilience and creativity, about seeing beyond the immediate challenges to the potential growth they offer.

The continuous cycle encapsulates the essence of our journey through this book—a journey that doesn't conclude within these pages, but continues in the lived experiences we each embrace beyond them.

CONCLUSION

A S WE REFLECT on the themes we've discussed in this book, we see that embracing the sh!t show involves more than just confronting our challenges. It is the foundational step of acknowledging where we stand—our starting point for growth. It's about facing the raw, often uncomfortable truths of our current reality and setting the stage for authentic transformation.

The next stage of the journey—leading a shift—represents the ascent, akin to climbers embracing new heights. It's here we actively engage with change, pushing beyond our comfort zones and leveraging our newfound awareness to drive meaningful shifts in our lives and leadership.

Leading a ship symbolises those moments of mastery and triumph. Like reaching the peak after a strenuous climb, it's a celebration of how far we've come. Yet, as we know, the journey doesn't end at this summit. Instead, it propels us into new cycles of challenges and leadership evolution, reminding us that growth is a continuous, ever-unfolding process.

As we step into the world, carrying the insights from this book, let us apply them to our lives with intention and action. Let's embrace the continuous cycle of growth as a lived experience, and apply the lessons learned to our personal and professional endeavours. This is our call to action: to take the insights and wisdom gained and make them tangible in our daily lives, and ensure that our journey of evolution is marked by continuous learning, adaptation and growth.

Let's carry with us into the future the lessons, laughter and love that have fuelled our journey thus far. Enriched with the wisdom from our past experiences and an eager anticipation for the future, let's embrace each new challenge and opportunity. This journey is a vibrant celebration of life's richness, highlighting our endless capacity to learn, adapt and thrive.

I am filled with gratitude for the opportunity to share my leadership journey with you. Life, like any great performance, is a continuous cycle of ups and downs, twists and turns, and takes us through the highs of triumph and the lows of challenge.

As the curtains fall, my hope is that you find inspiration in the triumphs and tribulations shared within these pages. May you discover the strength and courage to dance through your own leadersh!t, and turn challenges into opportunities for growth. In every shift, see the chance to evolve, and in every ship you lead, find the joy that comes from conquering the seas of uncertainty.

Life is not a finite script with a neatly tied ending; it's more like an improvised play where we are both the playwright and the actor. So, let's embrace the never-ending show with open hearts. Let's be ready to laugh, learn, and lead with courage.

Thank you for being part of this journey. May your life's stage be filled with standing ovations for the remarkable story only you can tell.

Here's to the never-ending show of leadership, growth, and the endless possibilities that await.

Curtain closes, but the show goes on...

EPILOGUE

A S I REACHED the milestone of turning sixty and celebrated three decades since my arrival in Australia, I found myself standing at a familiar crossroad, pondering the path ahead. Despite my accomplishments, a sense of unfinished business tugs at my heartstrings. It whispers to me during my morning walks, when I can hear it carried on the gentle rustle of leaves. Perhaps it is a message from the Earth itself, the vast expanse of space above, or the all-encompassing universe. In this twilight phase of my life, I've delved deep into meditation, seeking clarity on how to refine and fulfil my purpose. Only now, as I finish writing this book, do I begin to discern the shape of my commitment for the chapters of my life yet to be written. So, here I pledge, here I commit, here I promise, and here I aspire.

Yes, I've overcome considerable adversity, including surviving family violence. I've channelled my experiences into philanthropy, advocating for the prevention of domestic and family violence, empowering women, and being a voice for the voiceless. My dedication to protecting our most precious resource, water, is unwavering. Yet, I find myself questioning: Have I done enough? What legacy do I wish to leave behind, one that my daughters, grandchildren and followers can carry forward?

My pledge

Surviving family violence and grappling with the complexities of forgiveness and understanding have been pivotal in my journey. My father's transformation in his final days stirred profound questions within me. Why was he like this? Could we have done more to help him change? His reluctance to accept that girls could be strong and capable puzzled me. After his passing, unexpected feelings of loss emerged, prompting me to delve into his upbringing.

Born in 1933 in Azerbaijan, my father's early years were marked by tragedy—the Second World War broke out in 1939, and his father passed away when he was just thirteen years old. Sometimes I think I can hear the echoes of his footsteps as he trudged through the rugged terrain of his village, a young boy burdened by loss and uncertainty.

A year later, when his mother remarried, the dictates of tradition meant that he was torn from his mother's embrace and left at the mercy of his aunt's harsh grip. The memory of that moment lingered, the anguish as he watched his mother fade into the distance forever etched in his eyes. Raised as his aunt's servant, my father endured the sting of abandonment and the bitterness of betrayal. The scars of his childhood festered, creating a cauldron of resentment and rage. Despite his mother's desperate attempts at reconciliation, the wounds remained raw, gaping chasms of longing and despair.

In his final moments, as my father grappled with the weight of his choices, I saw beyond the monster I had known as a child. The once formidable figure revealed a glimmer of vulnerability and remorse. It was a fleeting moment of clarity, but gave me a glimpse of the good man he failed to become amid the wreckage of his past.

His legacy serves as a catalyst for my ongoing commitment to combating domestic and family violence. Despite tireless efforts and widespread awareness campaigns, the prevalence of such cases continues to rise. It's evident that a deeper, more empathetic approach is needed—one that addresses the root causes of violence and nurtures healing and reconciliation. Reflecting on my father's life story, I've come to understand the profound impact of childhood trauma left unhealed. My father's experiences, shaped by cultural norms and personal circumstances, led him down a path marked by pain and anger. Despite numerous attempts at reconciliation, he remained ensnared by the trauma of his past.

Similarly, the story of my husband's abandonment is a poignant reminder of the profound impact of early experiences on the course of one's life. From the moment he entered this world, he was denied the warmth and love that every child deserves. His mother, burdened by her struggles, made the heartbreaking decision to part ways with him shortly after his birth.

For the first fourteen years of his life, my husband lived in blissful ignorance, unaware of the truth that lay hidden beneath the surface. He believed that his mother was his sister, his grandparents were his parents, and his brothers were his nephews. It was a cruel deception, a facade of normalcy that shielded him from the harsh realities of his origins.

At the age of thirty, he embarked on a journey of self-discovery, tracing the threads of his ancestry in search of his biological father. The reunion with his biological father and newfound family offered a balm for the scars caused by his past, but the scars of abandonment run deep and left an indelible mark on his psyche.

Despite his resilience and outward bravado, the absence of maternal love has left an undeniable void in my husband's heart, robbing him of the ability to give and receive love in its purest form. It's a stark reminder of the profound impact of early attachment on our emotional development and capacity for intimacy.

As I look at my son-in-law, raised in the warm embrace of a loving family, I'm struck by the stark contrast in their experiences. It's a testament to the power of one's upbringing in shaping the trajectory of our lives. And it begs the question: Are fundraisers and awareness campaigns enough to address the root causes of domestic and family violence?

The answer, I've come to realise, is a resounding no. While these efforts play a crucial role in raising awareness and supporting survivors, they barely scratch the surface of the deep-seated wounds inflicted by childhood trauma. To truly effect change, we must delve deeper, confronting the societal norms and systemic injustices that perpetuate cycles of violence. It's a daunting task, but one that cannot be ignored. Only by addressing the root causes of domestic and family violence can we hope to break the cycle and create a world where love and compassion reign supreme.

Twice now, I've had the opportunity to share my story with men-only audiences, and the response has been profoundly moving. In those moments, I've witnessed the transformative power of empathy, as hardened hearts softened and barriers dissolved. I suspect that many of the men in those audiences carry the scars of past trauma, or have walked the path of redemption as reformed perpetrators.

I've never been one to play the blame game; instead, I believe in the power of understanding and compassion. By sharing our stories, we spark an internal enquiry into the roots of our behaviour, illuminating the childhood wounds and unmet needs that shape our adult lives. It's a journey of healing and self-discovery, and one that requires courage and vulnerability.

Moving forward, I'm committed to extending an empathetic hand to those who have lost their way. I want to work with perpetrators, guiding them through the process of rewriting their internal dialogue and finding the strength to seek professional help. Together, we can break the cycle of violence and pave the way for healthier, more fulfilling relationships.

This is my pledge—to stand alongside those who have caused harm, offering hope and support on their journey towards healing and redemption. It's a path fraught with challenges, but one that holds the promise of a brighter, more compassionate future for us all.

My commitment

My commitment to breaking the cycle of pain and healing generational wounds runs deep, and is rooted in the poignant struggles of my own journey. From the tender age when love seemed an elusive dream, I bore the burden of feeling 'not good enough', of being the black sheep of an already discordant family. It was then, in those formative years, that I made a silent vow to shield my future children from the same anguish that haunted my own childhood.

Yet, life has a curious way of echoing familiar patterns, and unwittingly I found myself drawn to echoes of my father's presence in my own relationships. It was a bitter irony, a subconscious penance for perceived inadequacies, and a longing for a love that always seemed just out of reach. The illusion of love lured me into a relationship fraught with deception and betrayal, a painful echo of the turmoil I sought to escape. The weight of guilt pressed heavily upon me, a relentless reminder of my perceived failure to shield my daughters from the scars of a broken family.

This guilt, a spectre from the past, trailed me into my new life, my new marriage, and the unfamiliar shores of a foreign land. Driven by a relentless desire to prove my worthiness, I embarked on a quest to prove my mettle, to myself and to the world.

It wasn't until my grandchildren arrived that I was able to truly shift the course of my journey. They offered me a second chance at redemption and generational healing. In their innocent eyes, I glimpsed the possibility of a future untainted by the shadows of the past; a future built on the foundation of unconditional love and unwavering support.

Thus, my commitment crystallised into a steadfast resolve to create a family that defied the odds, where love knows no bounds and every member feels cherished and valued. I orchestrate events, gatherings and holidays with meticulous care, weaving together the threads of our collective history in a tapestry of belonging and connection.

For my grandchildren, these gatherings are more than just celebrations; they are an affirmation of their roots, a testament to the enduring bonds of kinship and community. In their embrace, I see the promise of a future where love reigns supreme, where the cycle of pain is finally broken, and the legacy of healing endures.

So, this is my commitment—to nurture a legacy of love and resilience, to pave the way for a future where every heart finds solace, and every soul knows the boundless depths of belonging.

My promise

My promise to safeguard our most precious resource, water, is a solemn vow. It was amid the preparations for my first journey to Necker Island that I stumbled upon the stark reality of Day Zero—the water crisis gripping South Africa, particularly the City of Cape Town. The term refers to the day when the water supply reaches critically low levels—to the extent that municipal water supply systems are expected to shut down. Essentially, it's the day when the taps run dry.

In the case of Cape Town, this term gained prominence in 2017 to 2018 when the city faced a severe drought, considered to be one of the worst in its history. Due to a combination of factors, including population growth, insufficient water management and climate change, reservoirs were depleted at an alarming rate. It was a sobering reminder of our planet's fragile balance.

The plight of Cape Town resonated deeply within me. Water wastage, particularly in the realm of swimming pools, is a pressing social issue demanding urgent attention. The traditional methods of chlorine dosing, with their incessant demands for fresh drinking water, stood as a stark testament to our collective disregard for this precious resource.

Driven by a relentless pursuit of innovation and sustainability, at AIS Water we embarked on a journey to revolutionise the swimming pool industry. Our commercial technology, borne from a deep commitment to conservation, offers a beacon of hope in a sea of waste. By eliminating the need for constant water dumping, our solution not only saves millions of litres of water annually but also sets a new standard for environmental stewardship. But our mission doesn't end there. My promise is to amplify global awareness and champion the adoption of sustainable practices, one pool at a time. Each conversion represents not just a step towards conservation, but a testament to our collective responsibility to future generations.

Furthermore, I pledge to continue the relentless pursuit of technological innovation, driven by a singular vision—to enhance the swimmer's experience while safeguarding our planet's most precious resource. For in the convergence of sustainability and technological advancement lies the promise of a brighter future for all.

So, this is my promise—to be a guardian of water, a steward of sustainability, and a beacon of hope in a world grappling with scarcity. Together, let us forge a path towards a future where water flows freely, and every drop is cherished as the lifeblood of our planet.

My aspiration

In my journey of self-discovery and transformation, I've come to understand that true leadership isn't about dictating commands or imposing authority. My aspiration as a leader is rooted in the profound belief that as we elevate ourselves, we uplift others. True inspiration emerges from the depths of our own journey, from the luminous energy of our own growth and transformation.

Having traversed the full circle of life's trials and triumphs, I stand poised to reclaim the spotlight, armed with a newfound sense of purpose. My mission is clear: to take centre stage once more, to share my story, and to illuminate the path for others to follow.

At the heart of my leadership philosophy lies the conviction that true greatness is born from a steadfast commitment to lifelong learning. Great leaders, I've learned, are eternal students of life, ever eager to embrace the transformative power of continuous improvement.

For me, leadership is not just about action; it's a state of being, a mindset woven into the very fabric of our existence. It's about embracing the relentless pursuit of growth and evolution, both personally and professionally.

As I step into this next chapter of my journey, my aspiration is clear: to inspire others to embrace the continuous cycle of growth and learning, to challenge themselves to be the best they can be, and to lead lives filled with purpose, passion and possibility.

APPENDIX I

DISCUSSION & REFLECTION POINTS

Group discussion questions

If you have friends or professional colleagues that you rec-
ommend this book to, you may be able to form an informal
discussion group to share insights from the book. Different
perspectives can enrich your understanding of leadership.

Here is a list of questions to ask in the group to get your
discussions going:

Leadership philosophy:
What values and principles form the foundation of your
leadership philosophy?

How do these align with or differ from the principles discussed in the book?

The role of self-awareness:
In what ways has self-awareness influenced your leadership journey?

Share a moment when self-awareness led to a positive outcome in your personal or professional life.

Building resilience:
Share a personal story of overcoming adversity. How did resilience play a role in your ability to navigate challenges?

What practical steps can you take to build resilience in times of change?

Celebrating achievements:
Reflect on a recent achievement, whether personal or professional. How did you celebrate, and what impact did it have on your motivation?

In what ways can you incorporate more celebrations into your leadership journey?

Navigating the pitfalls of perfectionism:
Share an experience where the pursuit of perfectionism had negative consequences. How did you overcome this challenge?

Which tips for maintaining a healthy perspective on success resonate most with you?

Overall reflection:
Which leadership principle from the book resonated most with you, and why?

How can you actively apply this principle in your personal and professional life?

Individual reflection exercises

If you are not able to create a discussion group to further explore the insights in this book, don't worry. I have created a set of exercises and 'homework' to help you deepen your understanding.

Values clarification:
Exercise: Identify and list your core values. Reflect on how these values align with your leadership philosophy.

Homework: Choose one value to focus on each week. Journal about instances where you embodied this value and areas for improvement.

Creating a leadership philosophy:
Exercise: Draft a concise leadership philosophy. Consider the principles discussed in the book and integrate them into your philosophy.

Homework: Share your philosophy with a mentor or colleague for feedback. Revise it based on the insights received.

Change resilience toolkit:
Exercise: Develop a toolkit of strategies to navigate change and build resilience. Include specific actions, resources and support networks.

Homework: Implement one strategy each time you encounter change. Journal about the effectiveness of these tools.

Celebrating milestones:

Exercise: List personal and professional milestones you aim to achieve in the next year. Identify celebration ideas for each milestone.

Homework: Celebrate a small achievement this week. Reflect on the impact of acknowledging success on your motivation.

Perfectionism detox:

Exercise: Identify areas in your life where perfectionism hinders progress. Create a plan to mitigate perfectionist tendencies.

Homework: Journal about instances where embracing imperfection led to positive outcomes. Share your reflections with a peer or mentor.

Embracing vulnerability challenge:

Exercise: Choose a low-stakes situation to practice vulnerability, such as admitting a mistake to a colleague. Reflect on the experience.

Homework: Gradually increase the level of vulnerability in different aspects of your life. Track the impact on relationships and outcomes.

Leadership mindset vision board:

Exercise: Create a vision board representing your ideal leadership mindset. Use images, quotes and symbols to convey this mindset visually.

Homework: Place the vision board in a prominent location. Reflect on it regularly and make adjustments as your mindset evolves.

Continuous growth plan:

Exercise: Outline a continuous growth plan with specific goals for the next year. Incorporate learning opportunities, skill development and new experiences.

Homework: Schedule regular check-ins to assess progress. Adjust the plan as needed based on insights gained.

Storytelling workshop:

Exercise: Develop a short personal or professional story emphasising resilience or a leadership principle. Practise telling it with emotion and authenticity.

Homework: Share your story with a small group of trusted friends or colleagues. Seek feedback and refine your storytelling skills.

Gratitude journaling:

Exercise: Start a gratitude journal, noting three things you're grateful for each day. Reflect on how gratitude impacts your overall mindset.

Homework: Share gratitude reflections with a trusted friend, colleague or family member. Discuss the reciprocal nature of gratitude in building positive relationships.

Mindfulness practices:

Exercise: Experiment with mindfulness practices, such as meditation or deep-breathing exercises. Observe how these practices affect your leadership mindset.

Homework: Integrate mindfulness into your routine. Reflect on moments of increased focus, stress reduction or enhanced decision-making.

Community impact project:

Exercise: Identify a community issue or cause aligning with your values. Develop a small project or initiative to contribute positively.

Homework: Implement the community impact project. Journal about the experience and its effects on your sense of purpose and leadership impact.

POSITIVE AFFIRMATIONS

Morning affirmations:

1 I am the captain of my ship, navigating life's waves with humour and resilience.

2 Today, I choose joy over frustration, and I am ready to turn leadersh!t into leadership.

3 I embrace challenges as opportunities for growth and turn obstacles into stepping stones.

4 My positive energy is a magnet for success, and I attract opportunities with a smile.

5 I am grateful for the chance to lead my ship, appreciating every twist and turn in the journey.

6 I am a powerhouse, and my strength and humour light up the path for those around me.

7 With each step, I am progressing, and even the smallest victories deserve a celebration.

8 Today, I will sail through challenges with the wind of laughter in my sails.

9   My mindset shapes my reality, and today, I choose positivity, growth and endless possibilities.

10 I am not just a leader; I am a master of turning sh!t into a ship of triumph.

Midday boost:

1   In the midst of the storm, I find calm. I am resilient, and I am leading my ship with grace.

2   My journey is filled with laughter, turning leadersh!t into leadership one positive thought at a time.

3   I am making progress, learning from every twist and turn, and steering towards success.

Evening affirmations:

1   Reflecting on my day, I acknowledge the humour that made challenges easier to bear.

2   I express gratitude for the lessons learned and the progress made on my leadership journey.

3   My ship sailed through the day's waves of resilience, and I am proud of my achievements.

4   I release any negativity, knowing that tomorrow is a new opportunity for growth and success.

5   I am grateful for the laughter that echoed through the challenges, making them easier to overcome.

6   In every setback, I see a set-up for a comeback, and I am ready for the triumph that awaits.

7 As the day ends, I celebrate victories big and small, and express gratitude for the lessons learned.

8 I carry the lessons of the day, leaving behind what no longer serves me, and embracing a peaceful night.

9 As I lie down to rest, I am grateful for the continuous cycle that shapes my leadership journey, turning every experience into growth and laughter.

10 Tonight, I rest with a heart full of positivity, ready to embrace a new day of adventure and growth.

ABOUT
THE AUTHOR

ELENA GOSSE OAM grew up in the Soviet Union, and emigrated to Australia after its collapse. She began working alongside her husband in the family business, AIS Water, and eventually rose to the position of CEO. At AIS Water, she leads the cause of advancing water disinfection technologies for pools worldwide, ensuring safety and sustainability in our communities. Elena is passionate about protecting water—our most precious resource.

Elena's journey from a non-English-speaking immigrant to a celebrated CEO is a story of determination and courage. Overcoming gender discrimination and personal adversities, she has not only built a successful career but also uses her voice to combat domestic and family violence, and advance people and technology. She is deeply committed to mentoring her staff and the broader community, empowering women, and helping anyone who feels marginalised, controlled or coerced to find their voices and use them to free themselves and make the world a better place. Her personal narrative of triumph over childhood family violence fuels her advocacy work, making her an influential mentor and speaker.

With over fifty accolades to her name, including the prestigious Order of Australia medal for her contribution to manufacturing and community service, Elena's expertise and commitment to excellence are undeniable. Her diverse background, spanning performance arts to manufacturing, enriched by two university degrees, adds a unique depth to her insights. Through her unwavering dedication and love, Elena Gosse inspires positive change in the world, both professionally and personally.

Elena's greatest obsession is her grandchildren, who are the loves of her life. She is fulfilling her dream of building a big family where unconditional love is the foundation and her grandchildren feel loved and supported no matter what.

www.ingramcontent.com/pod-product-compliance
Lightning Source LLC
Chambersburg PA
CBHW030527210326
41597CB00013B/1052